CONCORD FREE
CONCORD
MA
PUBLIC LIBRARY

BREAKING THE ADDICTION TO PLEASE

BREAKING THE ADDICTION TO PLEASE

Goodbye Guilt

Les Barbanell

Jason Aronson
Lanham • Boulder • New York • Toronto • Plymouth, UK

Published by Jason Aronson
An imprint of Rowman & Littlefield Publishers, Inc.
A wholly owned subsidiary of The Rowman & Littlefield Publishing Group, Inc.
4501 Forbes Boulevard, Suite 200, Lanham, Maryland 20706
http://www.rowmanlittlefield.com

Estover Road, Plymouth PL6 7PY, United Kingdom

British Library Cataloguing in Publication Information Available

Library of Congress Cataloging-in-Publication Data

Barbanell, Les, 1941-
Breaking the addiction to please : goodbye guilt / Les Barbanell.
p. cm.
Includes bibliographical references and index.
ISBN 978-0-7657-0674-4 (cloth : alk. paper) – ISBN 978-0-7657-0676-8 (ebook)
1. Selflessness (Psychology) 2. Caregivers–Mental health. 3. Personality disorders. I. Title.
RC553.S45B37 2009
616.85'854–dc22

2009033227

∞™ The paper used in this publication meets the minimum requirements of American National Standard for Information Sciences–Permanence of Paper for Printed Library Materials, ANSI/NISO Z39.48-1992.

Printed in the United States of America

To those who would be too kind:

Remove the mask and you will see,
what you hadn't seen before.
If you are willing to embrace your past,
even you could ask for more.

CONTENTS

PREFACE ix

1 **SELFLESSNESS AS AN ADDICTION** 1

2 **THE ROLE OF THE UNCONSCIOUS** 13

3 **MASK OR MASQUERADE?** 29

4 **WHEN BEING GOOD GOES BAD** 45

5 **THE ILLUSION OF CLOSENESS** 65

6 **PRIMED TO PLEASE** 87

7 **THE PURSUIT OF THE LOST SELF** 99

8 **LIFE BEYOND TRAUMA** 109

9 **THREE RS: REBUILDING, RETRAINING, RECOVERY** 121

10 **ONCE A PLEASE ADDICT, ALWAYS A PLEASE ADDICT?** 139

EPILOGUE 147
GLOSSARY 151
REFERENCES 155
INDEX 157
ABOUT THE AUTHOR 161

PREFACE

At some point in life many of us have been or will be responsible for taking care of an aging parent, sibling or intimate who is ill or in decline. Or perhaps the dependent is a child, handicapped individual or an ailing friend. Being in any of these positions is usually motivated by obligation, devotion, love or any combination thereof. In another context taking care of others is associated with the career choice of a helping profession such as nursing, psychology, psychiatry, social work, counseling, physical and occupational therapy, teaching and religion among others. In addition to the financial rewards, the motivation here might be related to satisfying a need to be needed and/or the joy of influencing the life of another in a positive way. People who choose to give their time, attention and energy to others on a consistent basis either personally or professionally, I refer to as caretakers or caregivers in the traditional sense.

It may be surprising to some and even shocking to others that there is a far less traditional kind of caretaker in our midst. These personalities assume the role not necessarily because of obligation, love or choice of profession. Their others-first, me-second mind-set is automatic and is not based upon any semblance of a conscious choice or rational decision making. Instead, they are motivated by an automatic, unplanned, complex pattern over which they have very little, if any, control. Their selflessness and almost exclusive focus upon the well-being of others is more of a lifestyle than a benign, admirable character trait.

Their perceived stability, unreserved accessibility and kindness earn them acceptance, gratitude and admiration from almost everyone around them. With the passage of time however, those who benefited from their giving nature begin to feel intruded upon and controlled. Those on the receiving end ponder, "Why does she persist in doing things for me without my asking? It makes me wonder whose interests she is serving, mine or hers? I feel pressure and just don't want to be around someone like that." When rejections like these occur repeatedly, the self-esteem of the people pleaser begins to plummet and she or he is likely to become depressed. Suddenly, relatives, friends and intimates are stunned as the person they knew as being so stable and available becomes fragile and inaccessible.

The hazards of substance and other addictions are well documented; however, would anyone ever suspect that pleasing others could also threaten one's survival? What could be so bad about being someone so good? *The craving for the please addict involves an uncontrollable desire to give without receiving and the positive response of receivers is the "high."* The obsessive quality of addicts' behavior and the simultaneous avoidance of satisfying their own need states can lead to emotional emptiness, physical exhaustion and loneliness. In extreme cases the pleaser overwhelmed with obligations to others feels trapped and considers suicide as the only way out. Mental health professionals and nonprofessionals alike are beginning to recognize that the overattentiveness to others can often be worn as a mask to distract the chronic caretakers from deeply rooted emotional problems. Similarly, in some religious circles theologians are starting to accept a related concept that although giving to others is a virtue, it is not *always* better to give than to receive. This volume is intended to deepen the reader's understanding of those addicted to the welfare of others and the origin, purpose, rewards, and repercussions of the addiction to please.

1

SELFLESSNESS AS AN ADDICTION

This chapter discusses the nature of addiction in general, the conditions under which the character trait selflessness is transformed into an addiction and a full-blown (caretaker) personality disorder. The unique manner in which caretakers or people pleasers form attachments and experience intimacy is also discussed.

The addiction to substances such as drugs, alcohol and food for example and the health hazards such addictions present are familiar to the general population. The addiction to activities such as shopping, exercise and television usually does not receive as much attention in the media nor in clinical practice as substance abuse perhaps because the consequences are not as severe. (The current "epidemic" of addiction to Internet pornography is probably an exception in this category.) There exists a third type of addiction that is not generally recognized, yet is potentially as destructive as the others. I refer to this type of addiction as *trait addiction*, an overinvestment by an individual in a particular character trait of his or her personality. That person is one who "wears" a dominant character trait as a *mask* in order to conceal inner suffering, particularly the emotions and memories associated with a traumatic experience.

Trait addictions have the following in common with substance and activity addictions:

1. Behavior entails excessive craving, a substitute for attention, approval, intimacy and a variety of self-esteem needs.
2. Exclusivity develops through the belief the chosen source of addiction is the only way to fulfill the craving.
3. When tolerance levels are reached increase in supplies is required for "high."
4. The addictive behavior is a distraction from underlying psychological pain.
5. The motivation for impulsive behavior is blocked from awareness, so conscious choices and judgment are not options.
6. Overdose manifests in self-destructive acts and the demise of significant relationships.

The trait selflessness and, to a lesser degree, kindness in most social contexts is viewed as positive and socially rewarding. One definition of *selflessness* is "a trait of the personality that involves placing the thoughts, feelings and wishes of others ahead of self-interests without destructive personal consequences." This definition implies a benign behavior pattern that does not meet the criteria of an addiction as indicated above (1–6). By contrast, the following definition of *selflessness* does indicate the presence of an addiction: "a trait of the personality that involves placing emphasis on the thoughts, feelings and wishes of others to the exclusion of self-interests." The Selflessness Personality Scale presented in chapter 7 measures degrees of selflessness from benign to pathological (addiction level). The scale items also identify specific components of pleasing behavior that are the most prominent for the individual subject using the scale.

WE ADMIRE BENEVOLENCE

There are certain personality types that many of us would agree are obviously off-putting, irritating and obnoxious. They telegraph their negative traits and we seek to avoid their presence. For example, narcissists are unempathic, grandiose and self-centered. Obsessives can be tedious because of their rigidity. Paranoid personalities make us uneasy because of their perpetual suspiciousness and mistrust. Those of a dependent nature can be demanding and draining. Hysterics and overemotional types are needy and dramatic and alarm us at times over relatively trivial events. The pseudointellectual is stimulating but distant because of the absence of emotional expression.

The self-absorption and incessant negativity of depressives is overwhelming and mood dampening. We may have compassion for these personality types but usually do not look forward to being around them. Pleasers on the other hand are easier to be near and at least initially they are a welcomed presence. They rarely display anxiety or depression. They appear to be the opposite of self-centered and the only rigidity they display is their need to please. They seem to be the opposite of dependent types, rarely ask for anything and do not expect anything in return as far as anyone can detect. Finally, they make life easier for those that are on the receiving end of their accommodating nature. What could possibly be bad about being so good? A comparison between caretaking and other forms of other-focused behavior begins to address this issue.

OTHER ACTIONS RELATED TO THE WELFARE OF OTHERS

Altruism consists of acts of deliberate devotion without ignoring one's own need states. The act or series of actions are deliberate and selective rather than automatic and unconditional. By contrast, the selfless caretaker's identity is submerged by a lack of concern for his or her own welfare, an alternative that is not a conscious choice.

Compassion is an emotion that may or may not be followed by an action, as is the case with altruism. Compassion literally means "to suffer with another." The caretaker not only takes action beyond that but assumes responsibility for the suffering.

Empathy is the capacity to view experiences from another's vantage point, a form of listening that conveys to others that they are being understood. Caretakers listen, but avoid being exposed to empathy in return in order to avoid the closeness they fear.

Burnout is a state of exhaustion due to overinvolvement in activities that may or may not focus on the needs of others and may not involve others at all. For caretakers, "compassion fatigue" serves as a variant of burnout and is the consequence of the expenditure of energy directed almost exclusively toward others.

Masochism is the tolerance of physical and emotional pain and the acceptance of abstinence in order to avoid a greater pain. Masochists would rather be abused than be alone. Although caregivers are inclined toward masochism (self-deprivation of need states and doing for others until it hurts), their primary motivation is to avoid the dreaded state of feeling invisible that is typically a product of early childhood trauma.

Codependence is a collaborative process wherein two people reinforce a destructive habit or addiction in one of the parties. The addict is usually a dependent personality. By contrast, care addicts gravitate to a broader range of personalities (dependent and independent) to feed their addiction to be needed. Another distinction is that in a codependent relationship it appears as if the addict has a problem whereas pleasers do not appear to have any problems at all, a testament to the deceptive nature of selflessness syndrome.

IS THE CARETAKER SOMEONE YOU KNOW?

Thus far I have discussed the nature of addictions and how a person can be addicted to a character trait that can be transformed into a full-blown personality disorder. I have mentioned how by comparison to other personality types, caretakers are easy to be near and are commonly admired and perceived as emotionally sound. I have also distinguished the concept of caretaking from other deferential behavior. Below is a summary of the major attributes of the selfless caretaker personality disorder (CPD). In this context, I am referring to the addiction to please and CPD as virtually synonymous.

Caretakers

- Form attachments by giving emotionally and physically and routinely avoid receiving in return, creating an imbalance of give and receive in their interactions with others. ("You need me for everything; I don't need you for anything.")
- Are consumed with guilt and easily susceptible to being induced into feeling guilty. Guilt prevents the caretaker from taking any action (e.g., saying "no") that might lead to rejection or abandonment by oth-

ers. Accordingly, the conscious experience of guilt is a mere smoke screen for the insidious anxiety that resides in the unconscious of the caretaker personality.

- Are motivated by a compulsive need to be needed whether or not the receiver has any need for what is being offered. These behaviors inevitably lead to rejection . . . ironically, the very outcome the pleaser is seeking to avoid.
- Repress the need for pleasure, joy and intimacy. Their message is, "If I don't want anything I won't be disappointed; making sure others are happy helps me not think about my own pleasure."
- Become saturated with obligations that are both requested from others and self-imposed. The constant activity and expenditure in meeting obligations obviates the need for pleasure and exposure to being ignored or rejected.
- In conflict situations presume self-blame and are compelled to take undue responsibility for the problems and conflicts others encounter.
- Appear independent and self-sustaining and treat others the way they secretly wish to be treated with regard to indulgence and nurturing. Asking directly or indirectly for those needs to be met is perceived as emotionally risky.
- Deny loneliness and any reasonable state of needing others while presuming others have those needs, even if they do not.
- Conceal their desires and wishes and expect others to know what they want and need. The result is a

profound sense of entitlement and anger that remains dormant when they feel ignored.
- Rarely say "no" and withhold information from others (irritability, oppositional thoughts, anger, conflict, and so forth) that precludes authentic communication and meaningful relationships.
- Are eventually perceived as "too good to be true" and others begin to mistrust their motives because their actions deflect mutuality and reciprocity.
- Seem supremely confident, secure and self-sustaining in spite of a history that has damaged their self-esteem and enhanced their insecurity.

CARE ADDICT RELATIONSHIPS: REAL OR IMAGINED?

The attributes described above impact the relationships of caretakers in several unique ways. They shape interactions with others in such a way that they are needed whether or not that reflects the reality of the situation. They decide the agenda for which contact is made ("It's about you, not me") and the frequency of the contact (" . . . as often as I think you need me"). Of utmost importance is that caretakers attempt to dominate the give-receive balance in their relationships ("I give but never receive"), a subtle protective reflex to maintain control and distance. The receiver is in a position to either accept or reject what is offered but at least initially is oblivious to the pleaser's plot to manipulate the situation. The receiver's compliance then contributes to the effectiveness of the caretaker's efforts to remain emotionally safe. Both parties are unaware of the following: *It is difficult, if not impossible, to establish a true connection with another person without approximating a balance of give and receive in their interaction.* In this sense, most relationships care addicts form are one-sided and in the purest sense not real.

MATCHES AND MISMATCHES

The quality of relationships involving unresolved caretaker issues vacillates between heaven and hell, so to speak. For example, encounters between caretakers and hypochondriacs or those prone to psychosomatic complaints usually meet the needs of both parties in the beginning. The pleaser responds enthusiastically as they are fed a large "dose" of the needs of the somatic complainer. Similarly, when pleasers hookup with dependents, their daily dose of need-to-be-needed is comparably gratifying. Stoic types that include intellectuals and compulsives can contract a partnership with pleasers that contains a "clause" for emotional distance–a perfect fit and a sanctuary from the rejection care addicts abhor. Mismatches that may not begin at all are care addicts and paranoid types who are likely to be suspicious of the pattern of excessive accommodations ("They probably want something from me."). Independent, self-sustaining individuals, especially narcissistic types, almost immediately experience caretakers as intrusive and annoying. Pleasers involved with other pleasers are also not likely be attracted to one another or, if they are, eventually will clash because neither party is comfortable with receiving ("I need to give to you, but don't bother giving to me."). Individuals who are emotionally unstable and excessively needy can also be seduced into joining the caretaker rescue/savior (self-protection) program. That may be one of the reasons helping professionals are often prone to the caretaker disorder.

In the beginning of an employer-employee pairing the "perfect match" is a demanding boss and the compliant pleaser at the ready to give 110 percent. In my practice, I have encountered more than a few office managers who perform this way even when the employer is not particularly demanding. Their typical office behavior includes doing special favors, working double shifts when asked, accommodating everyone at all times, working overtime without compensation and never requesting time off. The underlying motives prevail: being liked by everyone all the time and a built-in "guarantee" of never being fired. On the other side, a match between a caretaker and an employer who is not demanding arouses high anxiety for the caretaker because of the absence of such a guarantee. ("The more you need me the less likely it is that I will be fired and vice-versa.")

These so-called matches and mismatches have the same fate in common. The probability of the relationship's survival is severely limited because the differences inherent in their respective biographies are almost always irreconcilable. For example, at some point the expectations of the somatic complainer or the dependent type will coerce the already overobligated pleaser into episodes of unbearable guilt, frustration, repressed anger and entrapment. Similarly, in the work setting the demands of the job made by the boss combined with those demands that are self-imposed will succumb to fatigue and the perception of each workday as a nightmare.

The perpetual deference to the needs, wishes and desires of others defined in this chapter as the addiction to please inevitably leads to emotional emptiness, social isolation, and the inability to form meaningful attachments. How the apparently benign, socially redeemable character trait selflessness can become so problematic and even dangerous is the subject of the next chapter.

Key Points

- In addition to being addicted to a substance or activity a person can be addicted to a character trait.
- Selflessness is the character trait that is central to the addiction to please.

- Excessive pleasing and the simultaneous neglect of one's own need states can lead to a serious emotional disturbance, the caretaker personality disorder.
- This disorder may be the most deceptive of all known personality disorders because it is difficult to detect, appears "normal," is seldom off-putting, and in many ways is socially redeeming.
- Most relationships for caretakers are imbalanced with regard to give-receive and therefore they are more an illusion than a reality.

2

THE ROLE OF THE UNCONSCIOUS

Why does a habit become an addiction to a substance, activity or trait? A simple explanation might be, "it just feels good." If you say to a cocaine abuser, "Your life is in the toilet," he or she might respond, laughing, "It is you who are full of shit. I feel great!" An alternate answer to the question might be that the habit is a substitute for an underlying need state. A person who feels unloved may consciously gratify that need by substituting food without the risk of human interaction ("I didn't get what I needed at home but the ice cream was always there."). A more complex reason why a habit becomes an addiction is that the cause of its persistence is rooted in the unconscious part of the mind. This addict's "blind spot" results in a desperate attempt to fill the void with an endless supply of substitutes and never the "real thing," an unknown at the time. Since the substitute is always insufficient the addict is in a constant state of needing more of it, whatever it may be. This chapter highlights the power of the unconscious in general and its specific role in the addiction to please in particular.

THE DUAL NATURE OF THE UNCONSCIOUS

Even after nearly one hundred years since Freud introduced the concept to the Vienna Congress the very existence of an unconscious process in humans remains controversial among mental health professionals and nonprofessionals alike. The archives suggest that those present at Freud's lecture (mostly physicians) might have wished to pelt him with tomatoes or other like objects, to express their opposition to such a notion. At this juncture, I believe it is helpful for me to repeat here what I say to caretakers in the early stages of therapy. I ask them to consider the possibility that they may not be aware of the forces within them that are controlling their very existence.

The unconscious has the capacity to block out painful emotions and traumatic events, especially those that occur in early childhood. As such, a traumatized person can be "held together," at least temporarily by its (the unconscious) influence. For example, a seven-year-old boy who witnessed the murder of his parents managed to cope after the initial shock. It seems reasonable to suspect that some automatic internal process blocked from his awareness the horror associated with that event. Was it some unknown unconscious mechanism that protected him from falling apart and helped him survive? If that is the case, the unconscious served a positive purpose at that moment. On the negative side, when trauma leads to too much blockage of emotions, those emotions can dictate the way we act on a daily basis, an extremely vulnerable position to be in. *The unconscious is "janus-faced" in that it both protects us from awareness of painful memories and emotions associated with them and at the same time prevents us from embracing and learning from those experiences.*

I first became aware of the possibility of an unconscious part of the mind while attending a course in advertising on an undergraduate level. The book *The Hidden Persuaders* (Packard, 1957) included a chapter on subliminal advertising, a marketing gimmick that entailed flashing a product on a television or movie screen so quickly that the viewer was not aware that it appeared at all. The idea behind the advertisements was to invade the consumers' unconscious and influence their behavior in a manner that would lead them to purchase a product that they would not otherwise consider. Government officials determined that the impact upon the consumer was too powerful and introduced laws to ban the process. I was struck by the powerful influence the unconscious mind could have on human behavior.

If we had to go through life feeling every emotion at every moment, we would probably not be able to survive. As suggested above, we seem to have a built-in tendency to edit, filter and totally block feelings and store them away for days, months, years, and sometimes decades. As such we are able to banish from awareness unacceptable impulses, thoughts and disturbing memories—at least temporarily. If we were not able to do this the likelihood of acting out our feelings would increase immeasurably and indiscriminately. Imagine an eight-year-old feeling hatred toward his mother for forcing him to take violin lessons not having the capacity to block out those feelings and instead placing a goldfish in her soup. Consider the case of the teenager who failed every subject in school as an indirect expression of his wish to break free from his overcontrolling parents. If he had acted out, rather than repressing those feelings, he might have packed his bags and left home. A middle-aged man may have murdered his surgeon if he was not able to repress his rage toward him for a botched surgery on his spine. Without the capacity to store emotions, a child rape victim would not be able to function in the presence of a man perhaps for a lifetime, the survivor of an automobile accident would not be able to drive a car after the event, we would not be able to survive the loss of a loved one, nor would someone who was abandoned as a child be able to overcome separations in adult life that may include an intolerance for anyone bidding them good-bye even in a social situation.

The natural ability to deposit and contain and retain emotions constitutes the positive aspect of the functioning of the unconscious. I refer to this automatic coping capacity as the *psychological immune system.*

The Unconscious Saves the Day

The acknowledgment of the unconscious helps caretakers understand that they did not choose to live their present lifestyle and need not blame themselves for it ("I wasted so many years saving the world."). That life-style was invented on their behalf by an internal process that made that choice for them in order to protect them from a lifetime of suffering. Immunity from experiencing such horrific feelings seems to be provided by an uncanny, ingenious concoction of the unconscious that is unrelated to conscious intent or influence. Therefore, self-blame and blaming others for the addiction to please is not only unproductive; it also seems irrelevant since care addicts do not choose their selfless lifestyle. Moreover, blaming oneself and others inhibits insight, confounds understanding, prohibits positive action and derails motivation and self-determination.

The Components of the Psychological Immune System

As implied above, we seem to have an innate internal mechanism that "measures" what happens to our emotions. It appears that we can move in and out of uncomfortable emotional states and that the movement is controlled from within. Closer scrutiny of this regulatory mechanism is a preliminary approach to understanding the addiction to please that will become clearer in subsequent chapters.

When physically ill we take action to restore a healthy state. We rest, take medication or in some instances have surgery and antibodies are in place to complete our recovery. When free radicals run wild within our metabolic properties antioxidants automatically activate without our direction to divert their path and destroy them, preserving the potency of our immune system and rescuing us from illness. We do not have anything to say about it–it just happens! Are we are also prewired for protection against psychological assault from the environment? Based on observation, never to be confused with scientific method, I submit that there seems to be something in our makeup that allows us to cope with emotional stress. I refer to this prewired adaptive ability as *the psychological immune system*, a complex, organized, regulated reflexive action that is set in motion by the unconscious part of the mind.

Below are the components of the (hypothetical) psychological immune system that interact in harmony with our biological immune system as an integral part of our ability to survive.

A. The Bodyguard of Our Emotions

We are awestruck when we notice the remarkable feats the human body can achieve. Cirque du Soleil is a combination of acrobatics, strength demonstrations, gymnastics, ballet and entertainment that draws upon the circus tradition. The body elevates, twists and contorts into seemingly impossible positions. Pilobolus is an art/dance form of extraordinary ingenuity, grace and defiance of gravity. It is an entanglement of bodies that depict different themes of life. Several bodies glom on to one another and, in effect, form an unusual sculpture that defies the laws of physics. Most sports fans are familiar with the way basketball players literally hang in the air long enough to switch hands before taking a shot. The image of Michael Jordan "flying through the air" is familiar to basketball fans throughout the world. Sports fans may be less familiar with athletes who compete in *Ironman* events that require an entrant to swim over two and one-half miles, bike over 110 miles and run a full marathon of twenty-six miles. According to Matthew Gibble, Ironman and physical therapist for the New Jersey Nets basketball team, those feats must be completed in less than seventeen hours to avoid disqualification. The world record for such a feat is slightly over eight hours. As if that is not impressive enough, Dean Karnazes in 2006 ran fifty miles a day for fifty consecutive days in fifty states for a total of over 2,500 miles. The human body is capable of amazing feats and unpredictable "tricks" . . . a kaleidoscope of variations and possibilities.

Most of us realize that in addition to the functions mentioned above, we have the capacity to contain our most powerful emotions and divert them from consciousness. The way the body does this is to convert emotional energy into an actual physical symptom (in contrast to a phantom symptom that is displayed in hysteria or an imaginary symptom as in hypochondriasis). The body has the capability to remember what the mind forgets and automatically store away intense emotional and psychological information. It may appear that an individual chooses a physical symptom rather than endure emotional pain, but the conversion is not a willful act. For example, an emotionally distraught individual does not choose to have an ulcer—it just happens. Once the body "disguise" is removed the real problem surfaces and in more than a few cases the problem is depression. Physicians have known for decades that when symptoms of a medical disease are treated successfully many of their patients begin to show signs of anxiety, panic disorder, an array of phobias and depression. Another way of expressing this sequence is that the body's job of guarding against the awareness of emotional pain begins to fail when the effectiveness of the internal protective apparatus, as suggested, begins to diminish. The case of Eric is an example of body guard breakdown.

Eric, a compulsive-ritualistic type, synchronized his watch with the clock in my office. He was precisely on time for each session and took it upon himself to end each session exactly when his forty-five minutes were at hand. He wore a three-piece suit irrespective of the season of the year. His eyewear invariably matched the color of his suit. He offered to tell me that he had twelve suits and tinted glasses to match each one of them. He consistently greeted me with a ritual by shaking my hand and saying, "Good morning, doctor." He ended each session with a similar ritual: "Good day, doctor." He had not missed a session in nearly nine months until one day he called in a panic state. He said, "I have to miss because I must go to the hospital for a hemorrhoidectomy." I recall reflecting that his feelings had to find an outlet somehow.

Valerie, a selfless type, began a therapy session with what seemed like a medical status report: burning skin, headaches, butterflies in her stomach, backaches and neck pain. Immediately following her list of symptoms she requested a second session for the end of the week. Apparently she needed more time with me and was anxious to confirm the second appointment. The following events precipitated her "body talk": (a) her mother returned to Ireland after an extended visit, (b) the week of her session she was not working, and, (c) she had a dream in which I rebuffed her and saw another patient in her place. The narrative in the session revealed that for reasons that are typical of caretakers, the excessive focus on others being among them, her body was telling her she craved the attention and love that she was constantly denying.

B. The Mechanisms of Defense

In recent years it is not uncommon for the American high school curriculum to include psychology. In that course students are exposed to the concept of the unconscious perhaps for the first time. This exposure is usually accompanied by a discussion of the mechanisms of defense: an automatic tendency that demonstrates the active unconscious and its role in protecting us from levels of stress ranging from anxiety to the depths of human suffering. This inborn, automatic arsenal has the capacity to shield us from destructive behavior that may include self-destructive acts. In addition, without these protection mechanisms self-esteem can plummet, identity confusion would abound, and meaningful relationships would be rendered impossible. The defense component of the psychological immune system diverts psychological threat in its many forms and enables us to attend to business as usual. A partial list of defenses is described below.

Repression enables individuals to banish from awareness unacceptable impulses, thoughts and disturbing memories—at least temporarily. An example is a person who internalizes intense rage in order to avoid conflict. This ability to block anger people pleasers believe they can effectively keep others from abandoning them.

Projection allows a person to deflect ideas, feelings and behavior away from the self onto others. An example is when a needy, dependent type, uncomfortable with those traits, attributing them to another person . . . "they need me," the frequent posture of caretakers.

Denial represents an individual's ability to block out an event as if it never occurred. This process helps a person conceal an incestuous wish or actual rape experience, for example, and "bury" the experience as if it never occurred. The perpetual focus on the well-being of others reinforces the denial mechanism.

Reaction formation is the capacity to defend against anxiety-producing emotions or memories by replacing them with their opposite. This occurs when a disgruntled employee compliments his boss whom he perceives as a "selfish bastard." At times, this defense in particular may be invoked intentionally. (Defense mechanisms are not always unconscious.) For example, selfless caretaker types become exceedingly accommodating and passive when they are aware that they are angry.

Displacement is an act of diverting a desire or impulse away from a primary source. Road rage, the act of uncontrollably pumping the accelerator while driving and screaming obscenities at passing cars, is a form of displaced anger, aggression and hostility. Another example of displacement is the honor student who indirectly expresses anger toward his demanding parents by failing every subject in school. Caretakers are more likely to replace, rather than displace, anger with guilt.

Sublimation is a defensive process wherein an undesirable impulse is channeled into a socially acceptable arena that is often, but not always, manifest in a career choice. Examples include a hostile person becoming a surgeon, a person with sociopathic tendencies going into law enforcement, or an emotionally deprived comedian sublimating his need for affection by devouring the attention he receives from his audiences. One view of the caretaker personality disorder is that the entire syndrome is one major sublimation of the indirect pursuit of love by being kind to others, a humanistic, socially redeemable endeavor.

Rationalization is an excuse, explanation or substitute that justifies behavior and covers up the true motivation for that behavior. For example, pleasers rationalize their constant availability by convincing themselves that others need them as much as they think they do. Defenses can combine in their effort to protect. For example, "I really need them, but I can't deal with anyone finding out, so I will act as if they need me" . . . projection, reaction formation, rationalization and sublimation.

There are other defenses that are not considered "classic" that the unconscious releases in its relentless pursuit to help maintain immunity from anxiety. One of these I have termed the *tense defense*, a person's inclination to become preoccupied with either the past and/or the future while diverting attention from his or her present stressful reality. This unconscious maneuver is common in therapy groups wherein interpersonal tension is predictable and at times unbearably uncomfortable. In such a scenario, group members will divert attention to past conflicts with their parents and others outside of the group, or shift the focus of the members to "someday fantasies" that entail future career ambitions or relationship goals.

C. Character Traits and Masks

The third aspect of psychological immunity consists of the transformation of a trait addiction into a lifestyle wherein an individual essentially becomes that trait. Jim wore the mask of athletic prowess (trait) as if being the athlete was his complete identity. He was saddened to learn at his high school reunion that his classmates remembered his athletic feats but acted as if they did not know him at all. Allison wore a mask of physical attractiveness (trait) to "get by." As she got older and her physical appeal diminished she felt inadequate in social situations and became seriously depressed. In an effort to keep people interested in her and stay in her life, Tara wore selflessness as a mask and became disconnected from her true self, her need states and her unresolved traumatic experience history. The trait of "choice" for individuals is usually part of their makeup that has made them feel competent, confident and worthwhile. *When a person unwittingly invests excessive energy, time and attention into a dominant character trait, that trait becomes the core of the personality, and the mask and the person become one and the same.*

The donning of a mask, as it were, is not always defensive or protective. Masks or roles people play are often necessary to function in civilized society and as such they have a benign aspect to them. On various occasions it is neither necessary nor desirable to be completely unguarded and open about the way we feel. It would be hurtful to say to a bride on her wedding day that she does not look good in white, even though we might feel that way. Similarly it would not be very diplomatic to tell the son of a deceased person, "I really hated your father and I'm glad he is dead." However, when a mask is worn to conceal emotional pain its use may be deemed pathological rather than benign.

In sum, the components of the psychological immune system (figure 2.1) are in place to protect us from excessive emotional harm in a fashion that is analogous to our biological immune system. Both systems, of course, are susceptible to ineffectiveness that can lead to physical illness or emotional vulnerability. Several factors that contribute to the decline in the effectiveness of the psychological immune system include attrition over time, serious bodily injury, illness or exhaustion, exposure to crises or traumata at midlife, breakdown of psychological defenses and mask "rejection" due to diminishing rewards. The case of Jason illustrates this system decline.

Jason, a thirty-eight-year-old social worker, appeared to others to "have it all." He was handsome, athletic, admired (especially for his empathic nature and kindness) and intellectually gifted, and he was a talented musician. In psychological immune system "language" he wore a variety of masks that concealed an abandonment trauma at the age of four. His coping style was extremely effective until he was diagnosed with a blood clot. He was hospitalized and became temporarily inaccessible to his patients and family. He was not able to pursue sports nor could he perform with his band. Jason had recovered from two suicide attempts before beginning psychotherapy.

When our protective systems fail to protect, we need to restore their effectiveness and rebuild their fundamental function, that is, to help us survive on a daily basis in spite of the inevitable adversity we all face. The restoration of the biological system, in most cases, is rest, medication, hospitalization and/or surgical procedure. The rebuilding of the psychological system usually includes support, medication, hospitalization and a range of psy-

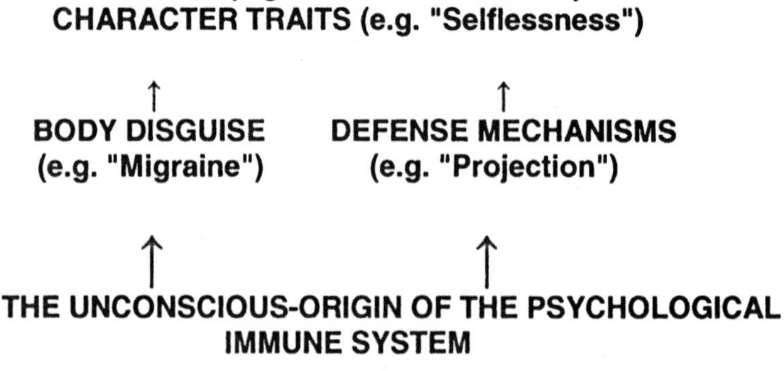

Figure 2.1. The Psychological Immune System

chotherapeutic interventions. The journey back to health begins with a proper diagnosis. However, the problem with some serious diseases, mental or physical, is that the afflicted person is not always aware he or she is ill or at risk. The caretaker personality disorder is one of those types of illnesses. The deceptive nature of the disorder is highlighted in the next chapter.

IMMUNE SYSTEM CHECK

- List your history of physical ailments that may be related to stress. Ulcer-prone? Vulnerable to migraine, chronic back pain, asthma, high blood pressure or periodic dizziness without physical cause?
- Mechanisms of defense you have used most frequently? Projection, sublimation or tense defense?
- Assess your most dominant character traits and determine your reliance on them. Are you intellectual in situations that require emotional expression? Do you rely heavily upon physical appearance, knowledge of the stock market, athleticism or your ability to excel at chess to deflect your discomfort in intimate relationships or in social situations?
- Are your contacts with others dependent upon your doing them favors or making accommodations?
- Are you known by your dominant trait(s)? For example as "the athlete," "the kind one," "the pretty one," "the singer"?
- Do you feel people really know you?

3

MASK OR MASQUERADE?

I have often wondered about the hierarchy of priorities in our free society. At times, when I reflect upon what some people choose to think is important I am not clear how those choices came about. Is it the media telling us what is important? Does financial success and its advantages overloading us about the importance of money? Why is it so important to be good-looking, sexy or famous? A sign of the times is the phenomenon that a sexy, modestly talented twenty-year-old woman with a shapely body can earn ten times more money than a surgeon. The possibility that her body and not her talent may be the reason for her success is no less than mind-boggling. Equally astonishing are the headlines informing us that some of the most successful and talented people in our midst have been hospitalized for depression or a suicide attempt. This chapter describes people who possess exceptional character traits that have provided social and cultural advantages. Whether or not these traits remain an asset is addressed in chapter 4.

CHAPTER 3

BENIGN MASKS HELP US FIT IN

Even those individuals who "ride the moral high ground" and espouse honesty at all times are reluctant to admit that such an ideal posture is difficult to achieve. In fact, striving to be genuine and open with others may not even be desirable and could be hurtful. We are aware that even people with integrity and good intentions are not *always* forthcoming with regard to their thoughts, feelings and opinions and certainly not with their secrets. Stated bluntly (cynically?) we are all "fake" to some degree for the simple reason that at times it is desirable and necessary to withhold how we truly feel. As comedian Jackie Mason said during a performance several years ago (paraphrased), "You don't tell a bride on her special day that she doesn't look good in white even though you might think that." Similarly, it is certainly not advisable to attend a funeral and say to a surviving son, "I'm sorry he's gone but I must tell you I couldn't stand the bastard." Contemporary psychotherapists stress the importance of authenticity and self-disclosure as factors leading to successful treatment. However, even in the therapeutic setting, presumably the safest of all places where trust is key, it is difficult to meet that ideal. The therapist may feel challenged, frustrated and even resentful toward a patient who consistently comes late, justifies not paying her bill and falsely accuses him of "abuse" for not returning a phone call of minor importance. Session after session, week after week, the therapist may think, "You are extremely annoying; it is no surprise that you have never been in a significant relationship and that you can't hold a steady job. In fact, you are not only driving me crazy . . . I think you are crazy and I hope you don't come back." Whoa, Doc . . . better keep that mask on!

MASKS: FROM HELPFUL TO HARMFUL

When we withhold the truth from others for the purpose of adapting to society we are protecting others and ourselves from conflict that may be unnecessary. To the extent that we do this, to that extent we are playing a *role* as if we are cast in a movie or play, *when the role and the real person appear to be one and the same, the role or mask shifts from a benign form of socialization to a pathological state.* When this occurs the benign mask the person has worn has become a masquerade that conceals deeply rooted emotional turmoil. The cast of characters includes a variety of personalities. The most dramatic among them are people with prosocial (socially redeeming) character traits that include intelligence-ambition, athletic prowess, physical attractiveness, fame-celebrity and selflessness.

The Mask of Success

The desire for financial stability, wealth and, in many cases, power has led generations of individuals to the pursuit of the so-called American Dream. When the pursuit is excessive, the option to succeed becomes an obsession. Workaholics are so busy with job-related tasks they do not have the time or inclination to think about their personal life and the unresolved issues they may have repressed. They are also reaping the rewards of their efforts while ignoring the possible repercussions from present conflict and past trauma experiences. Their blind ambition leads to tunnel vision and they become consumed with the next step on the ladder of success. Daniel Levinson (1986) used a metaphor to describe a depressed workaholic's plight (paraphrased): "He climbed the ladder of success one step at a time and when he got to the top he discovered that the ladder was against the wrong wall." Steven Berglas (1986) cautioned that the American obsession with success is an epidemic that can have dire consequences for those who hide their flaws and vulnerability behind it. Reich (1974) referred to workaholics as "living machines," people who apply their intellect and stoicism to the work situation like an automaton. These individuals have become what they do, and have replaced their true self, their essence, with a contrived role or masquerade. For these individuals the "drop from the top" can transform the American Dream into a nightmare . . . something to think about before thinking about becoming the next Jack Welch, Warren Buffett or Ted Turner.

Masks of Physical Attractiveness, Fame, Talent and Celebrity

Good looks, of course, are in the eye of the beholder and are based on subjective judgments at best. Those caveats aside, an attractive person has certain social, vocational and political advantages (style over substance). Talented and famous personalities also have privileges that noncelebrities admire, desire and idealize. However, how many headlines have we read that informed us of the tragedy and/or untimely death of well-known celebrities? We are regularly bombarded by publicity involving young starlets in rehabilitation from drug and alcohol abuse. Musician Kurt Cobain committed suicide. His diaries published in 2002 revealed the presence of "inner demons" beneath his celebrity persona. Actress Marilyn Monroe, who died in 1962, may have been better known for her sexy appearance than for her acting ability. The cause of her death remains controversial in spite of the recent release and examination of tapes of her psychotherapy sessions. According to published newspaper articles and research data, actor Marlon Brando's childhood was replete with family and personal adjustment difficulties and when he died in 2004, he had an assortment of physical problems, including obesity. Was his effectiveness as an actor fused with his ability to "be" the role he played? Did his profession camouflage early-childhood trauma?

In some cases the mask of celebrity is sealed tighter by cosmetic surgery that could be viewed as an endeavor to heal internal wounds by making repeated external (for example, facial) modifications. In spite of these and other alternatives available to celebrities to escape the effects of early trauma, they are far from being immune to its effects. On the contrary, I suspect they are at a disadvantage with regard to trauma resolution because their mask may be far too gratifying in meeting their self-esteem needs. "High" on recognition and idolatry (a shallow form of love), they are usually oblivious to the possibility that they are in danger of complete collapse. As celebrities become less attractive and the hero worship subsides, their market value is in decline. Suddenly, or so it seems, the scene is set for the surfacing of the horrifying emotions linked to the past and the masquerade is over . . . something to think about before thinking about becoming the next Marilyn Monroe, Elvis Presley or Michael Jackson.

The Mask of Athletic Prowess

In spite of the frequency with which our environment and the media project otherwise, it is not *always* grand to be a superathlete. Athletes are fundamentally ordinary people beset with ordinary problems that for more than a few may include childhood trauma. Similar to the personalities mentioned above they may have more effective means of distraction from emotional problems but they are not immune to depression and other human tragedies. Hall of Fame football player Terry Bradshaw's public acclaim and financial success shielded his depression until circumstances motivated him to seek professional help. New York newspapers reported in May of 2005 that New York Yankee all-star baseball player Alex Rodriguez announced at a charity function that he sought therapy related to a childhood abandonment experience. Bowling champion Bob Perry's rise to the top of his sport temporarily helped him cope with his childhood trauma experience until his protective system collapsed and he made a suicide attempt (1992).

It is not uncommon for the effectiveness of the mask of athletic prowess to begin to erode when the athlete in question has a history of childhood neglect or abuse. The catalyst could also be a career threatening injury, diminished performance levels, or retirement on the horizon. On such occasions the athlete, no longer exposed to the cheers of adoring fans, is humbled. Suddenly, the arena is silent and the athlete's illusion of invincibility dissipates. The rise above the crowd becomes an obscure memory and the former sports hero must now embrace the emotional turmoil that lies within . . . something to think about before thinking about becoming the next Michael Jordan, Martina Navratilova or Tiger Woods.

The Mask of Emotional and Sexual Celibacy

Masks keep a lid on emotions much the same way a lid is placed on a lobster pot when the lobster is being cooked. In a scene from the 1977 movie *Annie Hall*, producer/actor Woody Allen and actress Diane Keaton are in the kitchen cooking a lobster. The lobster about to be boiled alive manages to escape the heat and goes scurrying around the kitchen on its little legs as the panicky couple attempts to retrieve it. I have personally observed a lobster lifting the lid of the lobster pot ever so slightly in a last ditch effort to survive the intense heat. In a sense, we are built like lobsters. They have their two claws and eight legs to avoid, retreat, retaliate and protect when threatened and we have our own form of armor to protect us from physical and psychological danger (see psychological immune system). Similar to the lobster, we have a limited capacity to contain our emotions over time. The more intense the emotions and the longer we have attempted to contain them, the more we experience the need to release the pressure from within. Masks, of course, temporarily serve that purpose.

The abstinence from the expression of natural feelings and needs, as discussed above, is at times benign and necessary but at other times can lead to destructive behavior. Therapists, for example, experience emotions in therapy sessions but they are trained to harness and even suppress them while treating patients. As therapists we do experience feelings in response to our patients' narrative, and at times convey our true emotions, a process we refer to as "appropriate self-disclosure." Accordingly we do not practice emotional celibacy in the purest form (my apologies, Dr. Freud). With reference to psychotherapists, *restraint* rather than *emotional celibacy* may be the more apt term.

There are also those individuals among us that for religious, moral, spiritual and other reasons consciously suppress their needs for sexual gratification. Emotional restraint and/or sexual celibacy are human conditions that are not necessarily pathological or symptomatic of a problem. However, the mask of celibacy is active when emotional restraint or sexual repression is excessive and compulsive and serving the purpose of blocking a history of neglect, abuse or abandonment. Visualizing a lobster scurrying around the kitchen floor is comical but actions taken by humans when internal pressure accumulates can have serious consequences. For humans, the denial of need gratification to mask trauma can be a factor that contributes to the seduction of patients by therapists, the molestation of children by members of the religious community or acts of incest.

Multiple Masks: The Bionic Woman and Superman

Case One: "The Bionic Woman"

Vanessa had presence! She was six feet of statuesque beauty with flawless features. If she had chosen a career as an actress she would easily have drawn the attention of Hollywood's most prominent directors. She ran the New York City Marathon on three occasions and finished the race each time in less than four hours. She attended college on a basketball scholarship and played as a starter for her entire college career. In graduate school she received an A in every course and her master's thesis was published in a prestigious journal. She began a career as a personal trainer at a gym that she eventually owned. Three years after her initial purchase she formed a corporation that led to the ownership of five fitness centers that incorporated physical therapy and rehabilitation programs. Her hobbies included ballroom dancing and poetry writing. She won several dance competitions on a national level and several of her poems were published.

At age thirty-four Vanessa was living a life that those around her envied. She appeared confident, determined, ambitious, tireless and independent. She was financially stable, healthy and apparently emotionally sound. Her closest friend referred to her as "The Bionic Woman." From a biological and psychological perspective, it appeared that Vanessa's immune system might have been considered infallible and impenetrable. She rarely got ill and as far as she knew was never depressed. She came for psychotherapy ostensibly to deal with her mother's alcoholism.

A review of Vanessa's family history revealed years of neglect by her struggling mother and absent father, whom she remembers as always working. She spoke with anger that was tempered by compassion: "My mother should have never been a mother. It's not her fault. She was one of eight children and had a terrible relationship with each of her own parents. If it wasn't for my father's mother I probably would have felt I didn't have parents." The fact that Vanessa functioned on such a high level helped her "forget" about the influence such a toxic environment may have had upon her development. When she improved her ability to better manage the impact her mother's drinking was having on her current life, she ended therapy and resumed her productive lifestyle.

Three years later she returned to therapy because of two failed marriages to men who were neglectful and abusive. At the time she resumed her sessions she had begun a new relationship. She suspected she had made a bad choice once again and came for help having no idea why she chose men who had problems she could not detect when she initially dated them. It became apparent to Vanessa that she was on course for another divorce but could not leave her husband for a number of reasons (rationalizations). After three years since returning to therapy and approaching forty, the core of Vanessa's problems became clear. Her choice of marital partners and her inability to leave her third husband were related to a self-esteem problem originating from the traumatic *emotional distancing* and neglect she had experienced as a child. Vanessa reacted to this revelation: "Who would have thunk it? Not I, not my family and not my friends. 'The Bionic Woman' has a confidence problem?"

Case Two: "The Rise, the Fall and the Return of Superman"

Clark learned to walk, swim and ride a bicycle earlier than most children. His lack of interest in school notwithstanding, he was superior to his peers in almost everything he did. Clark was in his midtwenties when he began therapy. He told me that when he was in school (elementary through high school), he was the best athlete among his peers and superior to them in baseball, track, basketball and soccer. I couldn't detect whether he was being arrogant, stating a distorted biased opinion or speaking the truth. Then he told me he could sing like Frank Sinatra and dance like Gene Kelly and my doubts increased. His narrative also included what I thought was a far-fetched comparison. He said matter-of-factly that his girlfriend looked like actress Natalie Wood and that she was just "okay." When he mentioned that he turned down a part in the original Broadway production of *West Side Story*, I became even more skeptical about his sense of reality.

In the weeks that followed I made a mental note regarding his physical appearance. I had the thought that he could have been the offspring of one of the most attractive leading men in Hollywood at the time, Paul Newman. At that moment, for a split second, I thought maybe he had been telling the truth all along. I received a phone call from him one day asking my permission for him to bring a friend to session whom he had known most of his life. He said: "I know you don't believe me when I tell you some things. I would like to bring in a lifelong friend who will tell you what kind of life I have." Clark's request was a reaction to a statement I had made the previous week. I had said to him that if he believed that he was so special and that everything he told me was real, why would he believe that if he died no one would care. His close friend joined us and what he shared gave me the impression that Clark was not only being truthful all along, but being relatively modest. His natural gifts, his talent and his determination to be the best he could be resulted in a wide array of achievements. By the time he reached thirty-two he surprised even himself and discovered that he had a superior intellect. No surprise to those around him, he graduated college with honors and three years later had a book published. Clark had become a bonafide achievement collector and a "man for all seasons." Of course, his friends referred to him as Superman.

Although he believed that he had always received more attention than he would ever require, Clark felt isolated and alone. He sensed that he was stuck in a pattern of relationships with much younger women who did not satisfy his emotional and intellectual needs and that this pattern had something to do with the emptiness he felt. He would "take care" of his young girlfriends as if they were his children. The outcome of these shallow relationships was predictable; he said, "It was like starting a book from the beginning and already knowing the ending. At the end I always feel the same–invisible."

During the initial and middle phase of his treatment, Clark had mentioned his father only once in passing, quite an unusual occurrence. He said: "My father left when I was four and never returned. My mother remarried nine years later to the sweetest man I ever knew." I asked him if he remembered anything about his relationship with his father. He responded that his mother never spoke of him with the exception of saying to Clark, "Don't ever grow up to be a bum like your father." Five years into his therapy he told his therapy group about a dream: "I approached a man who looked like a hobo. These days we would call him a homeless person. I extended my hand to make contact and he turned his back on me and walked away. Then I woke up." As Clark was relating the dream a few tears flowed down his left cheek . . . only his left cheek. When I pointed this out to him he gave us (myself and group members) the impression that he was completely unaware that he was crying.

Thirty years following his last therapy session Clark tore his Achilles tendon in a basketball game. He had never been injured in his life and found himself on crutches for nearly one year. He could not work and could not participate in sports. He was unable to concentrate and could not write. He was in no mood to sing or dance and was unable to listen to music, another one of his passions. He spiraled down into a deep depression and made a near fatal suicide attempt. What happened to Superman?

Clark's "kryptonite," his injury, decimated all his masks in one fell swoop. He had insights into his caretaker issues, and his work on himself in and out of therapy was helping him achieve a more balanced give-receive interaction with others. He was connecting with others on a more intimate, real level and was in a meaningful relationship that had implications for the future. In his words, "The injury humbled me and I joined the human race for the first time. It forced me to let go of my Superman-rescuer-father complex and I stopped flying above the crowd." Following his recovery from the effects of his childhood trauma and subsequent depression, Clark's immune system was reconstructed and restored He was now "reduced" to being a regular person who was able to pursue a more balanced lifestyle without the necessity to wear his unique character traits (masks) for protective purposes.

The case histories of Vanessa and Clark . . . something to think about when thinking about the benefits and the hardships of being uniquely gifted or talented.

HIGHLIGHTS

1. Masks are necessary when ______________________.

2. A mask becomes a masquerade when ___________ __________.
3. Being exceptional is a burden when ___________ _________.
4. Gifted and talented people are at a disadvantage regarding the resolution of childhood trauma because ______________________.
5. Emotional/sexual celibacy is dangerous when _____ _________________.

4

WHEN BEING GOOD GOES BAD

The notion that it is better to give than to receive is deeply imbedded in our cultural value-belief orientation, especially during the holiday season when gift giving is the spirit of the day. This chapter challenges this belief and details conditions that support my proposal that it is not *always* better to give than to receive and that giving or kindness can be "worn" as a protective mask.

We usually admire people who can suspend their needs, wishes and desires in order to give to be kind to others. Individuals who display the trait of kindness or selflessness seem to make contact with others easily. Their accessibility, reliability, thoughtfulness and well-intentioned advice serve to enhance the contacts that they make. Webster's dictionary defines *kindness* as "sympathetic, forbearing, of pleasant nature or temperament, quality of character, altruistic, benevolent, charitable, indulgent and philanthropic." Aristotle considered kindness as helpfulness towards someone in need without seeking any reward in return. The action taken is exclusively for the advantage of the person being helped and not the helper. Other philosophers on the subject espouse that a truly kind person has no ulterior motive and that his or her interest in others is sincere and not considered manipulative, deceptive or patronizing. Kindness is listed in the medieval chivalric code as a "knightly virtue" along with courage, justice, mercy, hope, faithfulness, forgiveness and patience. Dante's *Divine Comedy* refers to "kind" as one of the critically important human virtues in contrast to the seven deadly sins. Aesop wrote that acts of kindness, no matter how small, are never wasted and that kindness blesses and benefits both giver and receiver.

For individuals rich or poor, well known or unknown, impacting the life of another by being kind or giving enhances self-esteem and provides a connection to others that is empowering and spiritually gratifying. Ordinary people, celebrities, philanthropists and political leaders throughout history have influenced the lives of others in a positive way and in doing so, it seems reasonable to expect, they experienced the satisfaction and joy that magnanimity can provide.

The humanitarian effort of Florence Nightingale during the Crimean War set a precedent for the nursing profession, as we know it today. She became known as "the lady with the lamp" because she walked through the halls of the army hospital carrying a light while, at risk herself, nursing the wounds of British soldiers. The lamp became the symbol for freedom for women to choose their own work, perhaps a precursor of the women's movement. In the late nineteenth century, Andrew Carnegie donated millions of dollars to various causes that encouraged people to improve their lives through study and hard work. He financed libraries throughout the world and subsidized construction of Carnegie Hall, Carnegie Mellon University and the Carnegie Institute for Research in the Physical and Biological Sciences. Mother Teresa, the "saint of the gutters," was a Roman Catholic nun who received a Nobel Peace Prize in 1979 for her dedication to the poor. Princess Diana of Wales, before her death in 1997, was instrumental in helping the ill and the poor. She exemplified that magnanimity and high position in government could coexist. Photographs of her cradling HIV babies and holding hands with lepers in Zimbabwe are well documented.

A typical parlor debate that will certainly not be resolved here is whether or not kindness and selfless acts such as philanthropy are void of self-serving motivation. Florence Nightingale was a heroine and the object of attention and admiration for the British soldiers. Andrew Carnegie had his name placed on many of his projects. Princess Diana received international recognition for her courage. Was Mother Teresa's dedication totally selfless . . . did she have self-serving motives . . . was there something about her that was less than "saintly"? Certainly caring for others reaps both tangible and intangible rewards and in most circumstances from a moral perspective it's good to be good and from an emotional stance it almost always feels good to be giving. Can being good ever go bad? Following are examples of ordinary people who gave to others and their plight.

THE DESTINY OF CARETAKES FROM EIGHT TO EIGHTY

At the age of eight Clinton's mother took him for singing lessons. By the time he was fourteen he had a modest income from performing. The "man of the house" since his father died he believed the money earned was helping to support his family. Primed as a helper and a mentor during his upbringing, Clinton became a special education teacher following his graduation from college. He was so immersed in the lives of his handicapped students that he crossed the picket lines during a teacher strike. When confronted by the union representative he proclaimed, "The kids have nowhere to go, and I am their family." Clinton continued to help students and his own family members into his adult years and all his beneficiaries adored him for it. At age fifty he had not had a significant relationship in excess of six months. He became depressed and sought psychotherapy.

Academically, socially and in the sports arena, Julie, age fifteen, was a role model for her high school classmates. She was scholarly, captain of the girl's basketball team, class president and assistant to the school librarian. She also had a part-time job after school. Her peers emulated her because of her maturity and intelligence and often called upon her for advice. At home, she was equally self-sustaining, responsible and helpful to her parents. She completed all her chores and helped raise her brother when her parents were working. She quoted her mother: "Julie has never given me no more than ten seconds of grief." Even her parents did not hesitate to ask her opinion when making a family decision. Unfortunately for her, Julie was rarely invited to parties by her peers and when she inquired was told she was more like a mother figure than "one of the kids."

Gary spent much of his childhood driving tractors and cleaning barns on his parents' farm. He became an uncommonly responsible child with very little time for play. The pattern of work first and play last continued into his adult years. He married and raised four children while working two jobs and attending graduate school. Although acknowledged by his family for being "the ultimate provider," he felt unloved and physically exhausted. He unexpectedly returned home early from work one day and discovered his wife having sex with his next-door neighbor.

Ashley was successful, wealthy and generous financially toward her family and employees. She subsidized her grandchildren's private school education and gave her staff huge bonuses. On one occasion she loaned her daughter $100,000 for the down payment on a house and when offered payback refused to accept the money. She appeared to be loved by everyone around her for her generous nature. Her wealth did not earn Ashley a Mother's Day card from her daughter nor a phone call on her birthday. In the workplace, her staff barely greeted her each morning and she was never invited to their special functions, including weddings, baby showers and other occasions.

Janet campaigned for her husband's race for councilman and he believed she was responsible for his successful campaign. He later became governor of his state and often expressed his gratitude to Janet for his successful political career. She also received accolades from the local church for her seemingly boundless energy and commitment to causes. She disclosed (to me) that she was not in love with her husband and did not find him even remotely attractive. "I have obligatory sex," she matter-of-factly admitted. The "thanks" Janet received for supporting her husband's political career was returning home from a charity event that she organized and finding him having sex with her twenty-year-old daughter.

Colleagues and patients and their families at a local hospital regarded Millicent as an outstanding nurse because of her dedication, energy and accessibility. She exchanged shifts with other nurses whenever they asked even when it disrupted her family life. She never complained to supervisors that she had the least desirable shift. She extended herself beyond anyone's expectations for families of her hospice patients. Her accommodating behavior resulted in weekend shifts that the other nurses did not want and responsibility for the most critical cases on the unit. She was inundated with praise, but did not receive a salary increase despite over fifteen years of quality service and superlative evaluations from supervisors.

Alexander was a respected, prominent physician practicing on the east side of Manhattan. His heavy caseload did not deter him from carrying a pager (before cell phones were in vogue) so that his patients could contact him at any time. His wife often joked that he must have been the author of the Hippocratic oath: "The needs of his patients are not only one of his priorities . . . [but] they are his only priority," she said sarcastically. His uncompromising devotion to his patients nearly cost him his relationship with his wife and children and adversely affected his health. An amphetamine habit that began in medical school continued into his practice. As a result, he contracted a kidney problem and died during a dialysis treatment.

At the age of forty, Amy's son Tom continued to live at home. After her husband died Tom became her priority. She cleaned his room daily and did his laundry. The highlight of her day was serving him dinner. It did not occur to her to have him contribute to the rent even though he had a full-time job. While cleaning his room one day she accidentally came upon drug paraphernalia. Without informing him of her discovery she "played detective" and somehow was able to find out the name of his drug dealer. Although she was sixty-three years old at the time she drove into a crime infested neighborhood at 3 a.m. and confronted the dealer. When she told her son what she did, he beat her mercilessly and she barely survived.

Tim, a financial planner, considered it his mission to help his friends become rich by making investments that he recommended. Whenever he was asked about his social life he typically responded, "Wall Street *is* my life." He was so preoccupied with planning for his family and friends that he literally slept with the *Wall Street Journal* underneath one arm and *Forbes* magazine under the other. He would put aside his hobbies and personal interests in order to "help the people I care about have enough money to retire." Tim's effort to transform his friends into millionaires did not result in close friendships with them. Feeling isolated and emotionally deprived he made several suicide attempts.

Friends and relatives described Carol as "the kindest person anyone would ever want to meet." On one occasion she gave a homeless man one of her nitroglycerine pills because she thought he was lying in the gutter following a heart attack. She was also giving in other ways. Psychologically savvy, worldly and politically informed she frequently gave advice that benefited those in her presence. The beneficiaries of her attentiveness stopped returning her calls and eventually avoided her presence.

Agnes, age eighty-two, had a dream in which she was a flight attendant being held hostage at gunpoint by a man who looked dark and sinister. She told the passengers not to worry because the man was only an actor. That dream encapsulated her lifelong pattern of placing the feelings of others before thinking of herself. Agnes's deference to the needs of others—even in her dreams—lamented that there was no one left in her life to take care of because most of her friends and relatives had died. She protested during a session: "I want to be strong for everyone like I used to be; otherwise, what's the sense of living."

Since it is customary to believe that "giving is *always* grand" please addicts anticipate (expect?) the following rewards: to be appreciated, admired, respected and loved, to have wonderful family relationships, an abundance of friends, an optimistic outlook, personal fulfillment and high levels of energy and enthusiasm. Instead, as referenced in the cases above, they are more commonly socially isolated, neglected, ignored and unable to form intimate attachments. Connected to others by what they do for them, rather than by who they truly are, caretakers ultimately and perhaps inevitably succumb to physical exhaustion, emotionally emptiness, depression and, in severe cases, suicide.

THE EMPTINESS BENEATH THE MASK

When an individual's lifestyle consists of accommodating others and depriving oneself–when giving is preeminent and receiving is inhibited–benign and admirable selflessness becomes toxic and is transformed into "the mask of kindness," a potentially dangerously condition that defines the caretaker personality, the *please addict*. Some of the risks are indicated below.

1. Other-focused behavior is accompanied by extreme self-imposed deprivation of joy, pleasure, intimacy and fulfillment, a state of being that is difficult to sustain.
2. Relationships bonded almost exclusively by giving are tenuous and doomed to failure because closeness usually requires a balance of give and receive.
3. The effort to accommodate everyone and the energy invested in doing so can result in physical and emotional exhaustion.

4. Sacrificing time and giving material objects (gifts) including money usually do not have a substantial or lasting impact on others if not accompanied by love, nurturance and understanding.
5. The avoidance of expressions of anger and conflict that accompanies this condition yields pretend, fake relationships.
6. Receivers eventually feel intruded upon and controlled by caretakers because they seem to "push" their need to feel needed and irreplaceable.
7. Advice-giving caretakers are usually avoided, especially those who offer unsolicited advice. Their gratuitous teaching conveys an attitude of superiority that suggests, "I know things that you don't and therefore you can't exist without me."
8. It is difficult to form a connection with individuals wearing the caretaker mask because they do not appear to have needs, desires or wishes and lack any appearance of vulnerability.
9. The tendency for caretaker types to ignore their own need states (they rarely ask anyone for anything) trains others to ignore them and take them for granted.
10. Caretakers have a covert sense of entitlement because of their attentiveness to others that they repress and they often develop psychosomatic symptoms as a result.

A Case Study—Laura's Panic Attacks

In many respects Laura was the prototype of the caretaker personality donning the mask of kindness. Her family, friends and coworkers viewed her as independent and strong both physically and emotionally. She was the "glue" of her family and from her description "a mother to her mother." At work she was a manager with an open-door policy and apparently was never too busy to provide her staff members a receptive audience. When anyone approached her with a problem at home or at work she was available to listen and offer advice. By contrast she rarely, if ever, approached others when she needed assistance of any kind. Her psychological immune system was at an optimal efficiency level. Like our lobster friend (chapter 3), the lid on Laura's emotions allowed her to function normally, if not admirably. Her body disguise was unyielding and she was physically healthy. Her defenses (repression, displacement, sublimation and projection) were fine-tuned–she rarely expressed anger and avoided conflict and displays of vulnerability. Her mask of kindness likewise seemed impenetrable: the word *no* was not in her vocabulary and asking for something for herself was never a consideration. Although receiving compliments made her mildly uncomfortable, Laura rarely displayed any signs of vulnerability and seemed to "have it all together." The people around her who assumed they knew her had no idea that she was on the verge of a breakdown.

When Laura was seven years old her father died. At age eleven, she watched her two older brothers precipitously leave home and sever communication with both her and her mother. This double abandonment trauma (technically a trauma followed by retrauma at a later date) created a situation that under normal circumstances might have rendered Laura increasingly dependent upon her mother. Instead, the reverse occurred: "When my father died and then my brothers left, my mother was devastated and I felt responsible for helping her to mourn. Even though I was so young I became my mother's mother." Laura generalized this pattern in all her future relationships. For the remainder of her childhood, throughout adolescence and as an adult, she continued to defer to the welfare of others.

As Laura entered her forties her capacity to repress her emotions and divert them from awareness by attending to others became increasingly effective. In effect, her mask of kindness appeared to be perfected and permanently in place. She remained active, energetic and immersed in all her activities. In her marriage and family life she was a stable figure and frequent peacemaker, particularly between her husband and her mother. As an executive secretary for a large firm she assumed a similar role: helper, mediator, advisor and troubleshooter. In spite of a lack of sexual activity with her husband and a secret desire to have a child, Laura seemed content with her life. Her pleasures included an enjoyable television program or cooking dinner for family members. At the age of forty-four, she was hospitalized for exhaustion, panic attacks and agoraphobia. Suddenly, or so it seemed to those around her, a dramatic turn of events—the helper needed help!

THE TRAUMATIZED CHILD— THE VULNERABLE ADULT

Can the effects of childhood trauma be so powerful and long-lasting? What happened to Laura that transformed her from the glue of her family and a pillar of society to a fragile person on the verge of falling apart? The power and endurance of childhood trauma is addressed below.

I recently visited the neighborhood where I grew up in Brooklyn, New York. It was a surprise to me that the apartment building (actually a project) was so small in comparison to the way I remembered it. I commented to my brother and sisters that by comparison, I wondered if our parents seemed like giants to us when we were little, and was everything they said and did magnified in its impact upon us. In the book, *The Magic Years* (Fraiberg, 1959) the author tells a story of a child sitting next to her father watching the sun go down. Amazed by what she saw she said, "Daddy, could you do that again?"

The impressionable young mind is unable to abstract, thinks in *concrete* terms and makes *generalizations* from everyday experiences. For example, a three-year-old boy who was bitten by a dog did not go near any furry object for several years, including stuffed animals and fur coats. In another case, an explosion catapulted a power line from the backyard and through the window of the bedroom of a six-year-old boy. When he got his driver's license twelve years later, Steven discovered that he was phobic with regard to driving for fear he would be "attacked" by another telephone pole or any similar object. At an early age, Jill, the oldest of three children, was frequently in a position to shield her siblings from her mother's violent outbursts. In addition, she "got points" with her mother by helping out around the house. In her late thirties she related the following dream: "My mother was hitting my brother and sister and I yelled at her to try to stop her. She pulled my hair and banged my head on the floor." As an adult Jill's role as protector and pleaser was firmly etched in her unconscious mind and generalized to all her attachments. Jim learned early in life that passive compliance was the best way to survive when raised in a "dictatorship." "To tell the truth made matters worse, so when we did something wrong we covered it up with lies. It was worth the risk because sometimes we didn't get caught." Jim internalized and generalized this approach to his relationships with women. He would avoid telling them things that he thought would upset them and getting caught in the cover-up only made matters worse. His third wife labeled him "a bad liar who always gets caught." Jim's response to the accusation was "I could never tell her the truth because she would get upset."

Laura, Steve, Jill and Jim were not raised in an environment they could trust as emotionally safe. In response, they "froze" their anxiety, fear and mistrust with pleasing actions and "carried" the frozen part with them into their adult life. This process may be described in several ways:

(a) A response of the immune system analogous to the physical science of cryogenics wherein a donated body part, for example, a cornea, is preserved for future use (transplant).
(b) The residue of early-childhood trauma generalized to all future relationships, and
(c) A projection of the past rejection-please response onto future events that are reminiscent of the past.

THE MAN WHO DATED A PENGUIN

There are many extreme examples of how past influences can impact current behavior. Fetishes, perversions and sadomasochism are difficult to explain without acknowledging past-present associations. How can we understand why someone requires being beaten before reaching an orgasm unless that individual has a history of associating love with pain? A dramatic example of association is a patient who was mesmerized by penguins he observed at the Bronx Zoo in New York City. Following the experience he began to collect an assortment of penguins: stuffed, crystal, animated and "singing." He wore an eighteen-carat gold penguin around his neck. He was proud to tell me he was first in line to see the movie *March of the Penguins* (2005). Of course, he purchased the movie. He visited the zoo nearly every weekend for about three months when he made a serious mistake. He somehow managed to get close enough and was caught fondling a penguin and was arrested. He was placed on probation and required to see a therapist. Toward the end of his first year of therapy with me he came to a session sweating from anxiety. He sat silently staring at the floor avoiding looking at me. He broke his silence: "I think I have a Lolita complex. Last week I fondled my twelve-year-old cousin and I feel terrible about it." About a month after that disclosure he had a dream in which his sister, fourteen years his junior, was dancing naked on top of a bar. He recalled having an orgasm while he had that dream. This patient's unresolved incestuous wishes toward his young sister were rooted in his early-childhood experiences observing her actions toward him.

His intolerable fantasies about his sister were transformed into his "fascination" with penguins in his adult life.

THE BLAST FROM THE PAST

The protection against reexperiencing the memories and effects associated with trauma is effective over time until the emotions begin to find expression in adult life. When this occurs, they (the emotions) seem to have a life all their own independent of the person experiencing them. As the trauma victim's previously disconnected feelings seep out without warning, they wreak havoc upon their activities, decision making, relationships and capacity to love and be loved. Like the lobster scampering all over the kitchen, the emotions are "all over the place" without focus or direction.

If we are fortunate enough our adult life represents an amalgam of past and present experiences, with the past having diminishing influence with the passage of time. In such a state, for the most part, we are able to perceive our *current reality* objectively and in the moment. An individual's *biographical (historical) reality* is more subjective and, of course, has its origins in the past. Unless an individual is in a state of regression (a psychotic state, for example), most adults function primarily in their current reality most of the time. However, without warning the current reality of trauma victims can be "assaulted" by their past reality–at those times, disaster strikes!

Melanie responded to John's request to have a talk about the status of their relationship at a local restaurant. They had light conversation during dinner and ordered an after-dinner drink. Then, he calmly told her, "I plan on dating other women." Melanie's response was dramatic. She described feeling cloudy and extremely anxious and believed she heard an echo from the past in her mind, "Stay composed no matter what." All she could say to John was "I understand" and they parted company.

Rudy was at a business meeting when he noticed that his boss's shirt was out of his pants and had a dark stain near the collar. When his boss started coughing without covering his mouth Rudy excused himself and started to leave the room. While he asked Rudy if he intended to return to the meeting his boss was picking his nose. Rudy told his boss to "fuck off" and quit his job.

Lynn, a high school teacher, related that she did not fit in no matter where she went. She referred to herself as "the gypsy" because she frequently changed jobs passing up opportunities for a tenured position and job security. At the age of fifty, her personal life was equally unsatisfactory and unstable. "I bounced around from guy to guy and never settled in with anyone. Come to think of it, you are my ninth therapist."

Melanie, Rudy and Lynn lived the selfless lifestyle. Melanie passively accepted the terms of all the men she dated. Rudy always complied with the wishes of his employer. Lynn continued to bring cake and cookies to the faculty room hoping that someday someone would want to have a conversation with her. Melanie was speechless at the restaurant because her mother told her to "stay composed," when she was a five-year-old child watching her grandmother die. Melanie filled in the blanks related to this memory: "My mother always told me she had no time for my feelings especially when things were bad and now I shut them down on my own." Rudy's strong reaction to his boss was related to the shame he always felt in relation to his father at the dinner table. "I never told him how disgusted I was with him. Now I realize why I changed my last name when I went into business." Her parents told Lynn that her feelings didn't matter. "We have to eat and that's why we work . . . [so] feelings don't count," was imprinted in her mind. She was not able to tell her colleagues at work how she felt about never being invited to lunch, nor invited to participate in faculty room conversations.

When a child is shocked by a trauma experience, as in the illustrations above, the impact can serve as a turning point that has the potential to shape future decisions and contaminate relationships. The psychological immune system automatically splits off the awareness of the event(s) by freezing the emotions and memories associated with it. The internal pressure, however, eventually (inevitably?) seeks expression in the form of dreams, bodily reactions, panic attacks, social phobia, agoraphobia or other means or symptoms. One other outlet for historical unexpressed emotions is a "blast from the past." These are impulsive, destructive acts that are the manifestation of emotions that were repressed since childhood. On the surface Melanie stayed calm (as her mother told her to do) but then overreacted toward John by acting out and having unprotected sex. Rudy expressed his shame and anger toward his boss that ascended from his past reality of unexpressed disgust with his father. Lynn remained on the periphery of life until she could no longer tolerate the loneliness and made a suicide attempt.

The next chapter focuses upon the deceptive and dangerous nature of the caretaker addiction and the central role of guilt in the maintenance of the disease.

REVIEW QUESTIONS

1. In what respect are we built like lobsters?
2. Why is it not always better to give than to receive?
3. How come the addiction to please is destined to fail?
4. What is the relationship between panic attacks and the caretaker syndrome?
5. What are some of the reasons childhood trauma has such long-term effects?
6. What are the three most prominent emotions that caretakers usually repress?

5

THE ILLUSION OF CLOSENESS

The presence of substance and activity addictions is generally more apparent than the presence of most trait addictions. We do know that it is characteristic of substance abusers to deny the extent of their habit until they are prepared to do otherwise. Self-deception, of course, is the trademark of the alcoholic. Deceiving others is usually more challenging for the substance abuser than self-deception. Addiction to activities entails a lesser degree of self and other deception, although addiction to Internet pornography may be an exception. It is difficult to avoid noticing when someone is shopping seven days a week or when a person spends more time being around a roulette table than in the company of his own family. Certainly, even some trait addictions are observable. For example, the compulsive athlete shoots baskets instead of getting involved in relationships, or the intellect plays chess or reads books to avoid awkward moments in social situations. The "grand illusion," the most deceptive addiction of them all, may be the addiction to please and the caretaker personality disorder may be the most difficult of all the personality disorders to diagnose.

Pleasers are completely unaware that their style of coping may be a cover for an underlying problem. Certainly they are oblivious to the possibility that they may be in trouble and possibly at risk. The receivers, the beneficiaries of their kindness, are equally unsuspecting of either of those two possibilities. I suspect that even clinicians have underestimated the hazards of excessive pleasing and that diagnosticians have been neglectful in recognizing the existence of the caretaker disorder. Of course, the please addict's awareness and acceptance of the disorder is a preliminary step toward recovery and its detection by professionals is a treatment priority.

SELFLESSNESS MEETS NARCISSISM

Selflessness and narcissism, at first blush, seem like polar opposites. Box 5.1 reveals, however, that those two traits are on several levels intertwined.

THE DECEPTION IS IN THE PRONOUN

The overall difference between narcissism and selflessness is that the self-referenced behavior of narcissistic

BOX 5.1
NARCISSISTIC PERSONALITIES AND SELFLESS PERSONALITIES: DIFFERENCES AND SIMILARITIES

Narcissists

Differences

Self-focused, seek recognition
Lack empathy toward others
Believe others think about them often
Haughty, manipulative and withholding
Usually ignore others emotionally

Selfless Types

Other-focused, deflect recognition
Appear empathic and caring
Believe others ignore them if they do not please
Humble and indulgent to others
Usually ignore own emotions

Similarities

Attachments are vertical rather than horizontal or mutual, need to feel in control
Require excessive attention and admiration
Overt sense of entitlement (expressed)
Covert sense of entitlement (unstated)
Exaggerated sense of self-importance
Variation of same: "They need me"

personalities is obvious and off-putting, whereas the self-serving aspect of selflessness is far more subtle, tolerable and admirable (until . . . ?).

The behavior of the please addict only *appears* to be about the other person.

In truth, "it's all about *you*" for the selfless one under careful scrutiny really means, "it's mostly about *me*." In that sense, a review of the difference column in Box 5.1 suggests that the differences are overrated and that the motivation of the narcissist and the caretaker is not much different in terms of the pursuit of self-gratification. For example, always saying "yes" could create an aura of kindness, thoughtfulness and accommodation. However, at the addiction level, "yes" usually means: If I keep saying "yes" I will avoid others saying "no." Although those that are being accommodated benefit in these instances, the ultimate beneficiary is the caretaker whose self-interests are served ("They couldn't possibly reject me if I keep pleasing them").

This subtle, complex disguise is not an intentional plot to control and manipulate people into caring (neither is narcissism). Instead, the kindness masquerade is a brilliant concoction of the psychological immune system to protect the caretaker from additional pain and suffering (rejection, abandonment, and feeling invisible). Neither the caretaker nor his or her beneficiaries are aware of this "unconscious survival strategy."

Michael was a doctoral student faced with a deadline with regard to the completion of his doctoral dissertation. He had one last weekend to complete the last chapter of his research project before his supervisor left for summer vacation. He had tentatively scheduled the oral defense of his dissertation for the following September, the final step before graduation. If he was unable to get the approval he needed after submitting the last chapter, the delay could potentially have been another six months. At the time of the incident that I will describe, Michael's wife was pregnant with their first child. After graduation he and his wife planned to move to Japan where Michael would take a position at a major firm. Obviously, a great deal was at stake on the weekend in question.

According to Michael's description, his sister Robin was the quintessential caretaker as described in these pages. On the Sunday evening of that final weekend Michael, Robin, their parents and Michael's wife were to travel to their cousin's house for a family gathering. Michael was racing the clock when he received a phone call from Robin: "I can't meet you at the bus terminal because I have this huge plant that I can't carry so I need you to pick me up at my home." This last-minute change would cost Michael two hours of precious time that he could not spare. When he received that message Michael was in a state of stunned disbelief.

Robin felt she was doing something good by bringing a lavish gift to her cousin's, even though her cousin's entire home had more plants than the Botanical Garden. When Michael (begrudgingly) arrived at Robin's home she rushed to greet them and asked them to wait while she gathered flowers for their parents . . . another kind gesture. In addition, she gave Michael a bottle of his favorite cologne for the third time in one month. Hooray for "wonderful" Robin!

In Robin's mind, she was pleasing her cousin, her parents and her brother . . . all for *whose* benefit? Her "blind selflessness" disregarded Michael's desperate situation. In session, I did not have to ask him how he felt: "She didn't have a clue about my situation even though I explained it to her beforehand. I can't wait to move to Japan just to get away from her."

Caretakers, like Robin, believe (self-deception) that the only way they can avoid feeling invisible is to be doing nice things for others. The others, her parents and her cousin in this example, are easily swayed by the kind gestures (other-deception). Obviously, Michael was not impressed.

THE CARETAKER'S "PSEUDO" CONNECTION TO OTHERS

The relatability of both selfless and narcissistic types is suspect because of the distortion of giving and receiving in their relationships: caretakers overgive and narcissists overtake. Both personalities give very little in terms of attention, love, affection, and so forth. For the caretaker the giving of time, attention, money, gifts, frequent phone calls, and so forth, does not suffice for receivers as a substitute for a real bond or true love. Without a balance of giving and receiving, is a true emotional connection between individuals attainable? When I asked Michael if he felt close to his sister he seemed shocked by the question and began to cry: "My whole life I thought we were close and so did everyone else and now I realize that's not true. The only thing she let me do for her was to drive her somewhere. If she had a car I guess she wouldn't need me at all."

The pleaser's contact with others only seems to be a real connection, whereas in reality the contacts they establish are superficial and emotionally limited. Mutual empathy and self-disclosure, two of the main ingredients in intimate relationships, are missing in action, so to speak. Yes, they are always ready to listen, but rarely share their feelings because to them being vulnerable and needy is too dangerous. Another factor that reinforces the unreality of their relationships is their outward calm, patience and "understanding." Most caretakers avoid expressing negative emotions (anger, irritability, aggression, and so forth), and being engaged in confrontation or conflict. As a result they show others a "false front" rather than a true connection.

Men under the Radar

The detection of the addiction to please is also related to gender differences primarily because men camouflage their trauma in a different manner than women. Usually accommodating behavior, including codependency, is considered a female action. Their please behavior relative to females entails a greater emphasis upon compulsive advice giving, the obsession with money and work or hiding their need states within the context of a career in the "helping professions" (clergyman, doctor, teacher, counselor, and so forth). Rarely do male caretakers recognize that their "strength" and "expertise" on behalf of others is motivated by their fears of being ignored, rejected, criticized, abused or abandoned.

Professionals in the Dark?

Since the publication of *Removing the Mask of Kindness: The Diagnosis and Treatment of the Caretaker Personality Disorder*, which I wrote in 2006, many of my colleagues have become familiar with the caretaker pattern. At the time this book is being written the diagnostic manuals do not include "caretaker personality disorder" as a distinct mental illness category. The inclusion, perhaps, could diminish the "mystery" surrounding this illness and facilitate its detection and diagnosis. The more traditional diagnostic categories, of course, are much more familiar to clinicians, the lay public and insurance companies.

Guilt as a Smoke Screen for Anxiety

Guilt, of course, can be viewed as a "positive emotion" that deters offensive and antisocial behavior. For example, if the main character in the movie *Silence of the Lambs* had any sense of guilt he wouldn't have been referred to as "Hannibal the Cannibal." However, for the care addict guilt serves another purpose that is "negative" and ultimately destructive. In a mythical court of human relations when the please addict is accused of deception, the jury determines that *guilt* has been his or her partner in crime. The "charge" is conspiracy to avoid the truth because the truth is too painful emotionally. Self-blame and grandiosity ("Everything that goes wrong in relationships is my fault and it's my responsibility to fix it") may be deemed coconspirators, if you will. Caretakers live and breathe self-imposed guilt: a creative if not brilliant concoction of the immune system that serves as a ploy to avoid (abandonment/abuse) anxiety, neutralize anger and minimize conflict–a clever plot to maintain contact with others and avoid feeling alone and empty. Stated another way, guilt is a conscious experience in most cases that protects us from experiencing a more dreaded emotion, intense anxiety. The guilt is intended to stop the action that would create the anxiety. For example, Alice asked Melissa to take her to the airport at 5 a.m. in spite of the fact that nurse Melissa worked a double shift the day before. Melissa felt badly (*guilt*) thinking about saying "no." She was not aware of her *anxiety* about losing the friendship.

All-or-nothing thinking is a variation of the rationalization-guilt dynamic: "How can I have any pleasure in my life while my daughter is in jail?" Here's another favorite: "I had a great life with my husband before he died. I then married an abusive man. How could I enjoy the rest of my life when someone whom I loved is dead?" This dynamic is based on the illogical premise that any form of self-gratification is not possible when someone else has suffered or died. (Translation: "I found another way of not thinking about my abandonment issues.")

When caretakers are asked to comply with someone's wishes and consistently say "yes," but secretly feel "no," the compliance is almost always rooted in guilt and the grandiose assumption that if they didn't comply the other person could not otherwise manage and, worse, their world would fall apart ("without me"). When something does go wrong self-blame and responsibility prevail and the caretaker is available to save the day. Who are the real beneficiaries of these benevolent acts, the giver or the receiver?

Jennifer wore the mask of kindness every time someone asked her for a favor and even when they did not. By unwittingly shaping her relationships so that others needed her, she guaranteed their eternal presence. As a result, her "obligation list" so far exceeded her pleasure experiences that her body could no longer endure the strain and her body disguise (see psychological immunity) began to breakdown. Her actions toward others on the outside conflicted with her feelings on the inside creating symptoms she could not tolerate. Jennifer had to be hospitalized for migraine headaches.

DO CARETAKERS REALLY CARE?

The caretaker's elaborate system of maintaining contact and avoiding feeling invisible, as discussed above, is subtle and difficult to detect. Yet somehow, someway and at some point in time, they are either taken for granted, avoided, rejected and, indeed, abandoned, the very action they shaped a lifestyle to avoid. Can others see through the mask? How does it happen that such good people end up being treated so badly? The frequent acts of giving without being asked, in combination with their refusal to receive, with the passage of time arouse the suspicion that such kindness is too good to be true. The persistence of the giver begins to feel like an endless cascade of demands. Eventually, others are provoked into feeling irritable and controlled. To make matters worse, what is offered is usually the opposite of what others need. For example, wealthy caretaker types give money or gifts when what is needed is emotional attentiveness and a true connection. Are the grandchildren happy to see their grandmother because she is bringing them presents, or because they enjoy having fun and talking with her? Energetic caretakers extend themselves beyond expectations, but may not be warm, considerate or affectionate. The provider works several jobs, pays the bills and provides security for the family. However, when the family is at the dinner table he is tired and reluctant to share anything about himself or his feelings, an emotionally safe haven for his wounded soul.

Giving with an underlying self-serving purpose, keeping up the imbalance of give and receive, and providing substitutes for what others in their surroundings really need reinforce the illusion of closeness that prevents a true connection to oneself that ultimately alienates others. Caretaker personalities have perfected the capacity to be close to others while at the same time remain at an emotional distance from them . . . a distance that is inevitably transmitted to others. The "vertical attachments" they form (as opposed to equal or "horizontal") place them in the emotionally safe position they must preserve. *In the last analysis, caretakers may genuinely care for others but can only give what they are capable of giving at the time. It may not be what people need from them but until they are released from their toxic past it's the best they can do. In that sense they deserve our compassion and not judgment or criticism.*

The emotions of care addicts are so blocked by the trauma protection (alarm) system that they are in a state of *emotional constipation* and may not be able to express what they think they ought to be expressing. Their effort to give emotionally is typically so restrained that they are relegated to give substitutes for what others really need from them. The substitutes, disguised expression of love—gifts, accommodations, favors, and so on—are insufficient for the giver and receiver. The giver wants to express affection and love, but cannot while immersed in the caretaker syndrome. As is the case in any addiction, one of the reasons an addiction is an addiction is because the substitute inevitably fails to fill the original craving. If the behavior of care addicts is manipulative, I would suggest it is usually not rooted in conscious intent, but instead it is related to the emotional constipation referred to above. Because of this relational limitation, care addicts (see below) are often rejected without compassion, a state of being that forces a desperate desire to maintain the distant vertical position, even within the confines of presumably the safest of all places—the office of the therapist.

Sara: I am so lucky that I was ready to talk to you and what an amazing thing that you know exactly what's wrong with me. It took long enough for me to get here and I know I will be your patient for a long time.

Me: We certainly have work ahead of us.

(Patient continually praises me for my interventions and style. Over the course of six months refers three patients and repeats in session the testimonial she gave each one about my abilities as a therapist. She brings gifts on several occasions, especially holidays.)

Sara: I have told you things I never told anyone in my entire life and now I have a dream to share that I can't believe I am going to tell you. This dream overwhelmed me and I was close to a breakdown. I almost called you.

Me: Any thoughts about why you didn't?

Sara: I know you have other patients and I didn't want to burden you.

(Dream is discussed.)

Sara: I was wondering (hesitates), oh, never mind. Okay, I was wondering if I could have a second session every week. I know I need it.

(I give her an appointment for a second session.)

For over one month she kept scheduling the second session and canceling. She also cancelled several of her regular appointments at the last minute. She lapsed in her payments and twice gave checks that were returned for nonpayment. Finally, she called and left a cryptic message about her next cancellation. She did not return to therapy.

What happened? Sara had shaped a vertical position in her relationship with me, a position that she automatically established with others outside of therapy. She kept me under her control and in place by relating to me as if I needed her . . . her compliments, gifts, money, referrals and overall presence. She inadvertently slipped out of the vertical position when she had the dream and realized that *she* needed *me*. When she began to be aware of her dependent side ("I almost called you") she panicked.

What happened between Sara and myself is a template of what typically happens between caretakers and their "victims." At first, it is easy to be seduced by their generosity and its various forms–gifts, praise, kindness, accommodations, selflessness, and so forth–as long as the receiver is cooperative the relationship is "safe" and quite possibly the receiver believes the pleaser is a caring person. On the occasion that the vertical position is threatened the relationship is destroyed. Receivers feel pressured, controlled and not cared about in any intimate manner and reject the caretaker, or alternatively the caretaker becomes aware of needing the receiver and retreats, as Sara did. The caretaker without supplies is like the heroine addict who is unable to have a "fix." When this scenario occurs the caretaker is extremely vulnerable and in severe cases becomes a suicide risk. (Sara eventually returned to therapy after being hospitalized for a suicide attempt.)

In sum, the masquerade is over when

1. A lifetime of deference to others, although it provided a safe haven from suffering, is not fulfilling.

2. Giving without receiving is irritating to others who feel pressured and controlled by it.
3. The mask of kindness fails in its mission to maintain contact with others who do not return phone calls and in general seem to disappear for no apparent reason.
4. Associations with family members, friends and intimates are limited and fake.
5. The rewards of selflessness are far outweighed by emotional emptiness, mental and physical exhaustion and the trapped feeling that results from constantly being available to others and taking responsibility for their welfare (since childhood?).
6. No one reciprocates nor does anyone care. Did they see through the mask?
7. The torrent of emotions that were frozen in time break through and flood the collapsed system, and the original event and the emotions associated with it rise to the surface.

UNDERNEATH THE MASK

The relentless though misdirected effort to connect without anxiety eventually yields diminishing returns. At the end of the day caretakers are not only physically and emotionally drained; they are disillusioned by the lack of responsiveness they receive and they are running out of the "supplies" others have given them. Others have ignored them either part of the time or permanently. They became aware of needing others and abruptly slipped into seclusion. They took a risk and did ask for something and got turned down leading them to retreat into seclusion. Their vehicles for caring such as false empathy, limited affection and sharing resulted in little or no empathy or consideration in return. Moreover, unlike the enabler in a codependent relationship, caretakers tried to enable capable, independent people who resented it and pushed them away. Alas, they remain in silence expecting others to know what they need without asking similar to what they have done. They harbor a deep resentment and sense of entitlement for all they have done without directly asking for anything in return. Without an appropriate outlet, like the lobster in the pot they are trapped and must find a way out.

PSYCHOTHERAPISTS WITH AN ADDICTION TO PLEASE

The presence of care addicts is abundant in the helping professions that include psychologists, nurses, physicians, priests, rabbis, counselors, teachers, social workers and others. The "doctor mask" can serve as a convenient, prestigious, subtle escape from past and present suffering. The vertical position for therapists, for example, helps maintain proper boundaries with patients; however, the therapist with the selfless addiction may use those boundaries for "covert caretaker operations." The following compares the emotional state of therapists with and without caretaker disorder.

Benign States

- Therapist's personal growth and healing is enhanced by self-reflection during patient narrative.
- Attention to patients is appropriate and all encompassing.
- Work is a source of self-esteem.
- Responses are empathic and include self-disclosure.
- The "person" of the therapist is exposed rather than hidden.
- Therapist-patient boundaries are upheld.
- Patient autonomy is encouraged and reinforced.
- In-between contact from patients is selective rather than indiscriminate.
- Range and depth of emotional expression is not restricted.
- Contract issues (fees, schedule, missed sessions, and so forth) discussed openly.
- Therapist intervention activity is random and calm.
- Intellectualizing is secondary to genuinely relating with patients.
- Patient adulation is accepted as source of satisfaction.
- Therapist is clear about separation of role and self.
- Rescue fantasies are under control.
- Terminations and missed sessions are responded to in a professional manner.
- Reactions to patient's emotional/sexual celibacy are neutral and objective.
- Therapist maintains balanced lifestyle of which therapy work is a part.

Pathological States

- Personal growth is restricted due to overfocus on work and patients.
- Attentiveness to patients is excessive and inappropriate.
- Self-esteem is dependent upon success or failure with patients.
- Responses to patients are disingenuous and pseudo-empathic.
- Therapist adheres (hides behind) strict role demarcation.
- Boundaries are permeable and vulnerable to exploitation.
- Dependency is fostered rather than discouraged.
- Contact is indulgent and gratuitous.
- Emotional expressions are restricted in sessions.
- Therapist is lenient with contract matters.
- Therapist is unusually talkative, anxious and active.
- Interpretation and analysis (intellectualizing) are used excessively.
- Giving to patients is superficial and not characterized by caring or warmth.
- Patient adulation is a substitute for feeling loved.
- Therapist role and real person are merged in and out of office setting.
- Rescue fantasies meet therapist's not patient's self-esteem needs.

- Therapist is overanxious regarding missed sessions, terminations due to abandonment issues.
- Therapist reacts to patient's repression of needs by wishing to respond to them or sexually acting out.
- Therapist overworks, experiencing burnout, exhaustion as obligations to patients and others increase.

The research regarding the outcome of psychotherapy, irrespective of the nature of the psychological complaint, has revealed consistently that the relationship with the therapist and patient is the major determining factor affecting patient overcome. The emergence of "relational analysis" upon the psychotherapy landscape in the late 1980s emphasizes the interpersonal dimension of the therapeutic dyad. Self-disclosure, empathy, mutuality, authenticity, horizontal relating and the cocreation of a safe, trusting environment are the hallmarks of the relational approach. "Repair" of early faulty relations (especially trauma) with significant others in the here and now with the therapist is the relational equivalent of recovery or "cure." This orientation is particularly suitable for the addiction to please because of the emphasis on the real person of the therapist, a counterpoint to role-playing and distancing forms of contact that are central to other therapeutic orientations. The therapist who has symptoms of the addiction to please is prone to re-create the trauma their caretaker patients experienced in early life . . . a potentially hazardous scenario.

CHAPTER 5

TRUTH AND CONSEQUENCES

The lifestyle of selflessness had succeeded in providing therapists and other caretakers with marginal contact with others at best, a state of affairs that was designed to provide safety from the reoccurrences of crisis and trauma. The immune system selected the mask of kindness as a shield from these events and the emotions associated with them. As a result, selfless personalities spend most of their lives functioning in a world without "thank you," "I miss you," "I look forward to seeing you," "I'm worried about you," and "I love you." For the survival reasons mentioned repeatedly above, they are compelled to act as if others have those needs and they do not. The truth is the needs of caretakers are not only "normal," but excessive because they have been repressed, denied, displaced, sublimated and projected onto others. However, when caretakers are in a position to embrace these truths the hope for recovery from the addiction to please is enhanced (see treatment section). The case of William underscores the potential danger of the caretaker personality disorder.

William, a forty-five-year-old physician, acknowledged by his peers as "the surgeon of surgeons," was chief of staff at a major New York hospital. Several of his books were required reading for interns at the hospital. He was always available to his staff and his patients. Even during his therapy sessions he responded to his pager. His personal life appeared to be satisfactory. He was wealthy and provided a "life of security and luxury" for his wife, children and extended family. However, he was usually not available to participate in many family functions. He rarely socialized and his friendships were limited to his frequently giving them unsolicited medical advice. His patients needed him, his friends needed him and his family needed him. At his request, I agreed to have his wife join us for a session. She said quite matter-of-factly, He is not only devoted to his patients; they are his life. He doesn't seem to need anything from us." I asked William how he felt about his wife's comment. He answered abruptly, "I have to perform surgery in four hours and you ask me how I feel about something. How would I be able to perform surgery if I got into feeling mode?"

Several months after beginning therapy, William, overworked, overcommitted and emotionally and physically exhausted, had a stroke that nearly ended his life. He recovered satisfactorily but in the aftermath became severely depressed. When he returned to therapy it seemed that his "mask" was gone. He was not carrying a pager and appeared less stoic, more humble, vulnerable and emotional than in the past. He cried for the first time in his adult life. "Confined to a hospital bed I found myself in a state where I was of no use to anyone. I couldn't respond when my patients needed me. After one week I realized how few visitors and phone calls I had. My wife told me a patient called and wanted me to complete a Medicare form even though the patient knew I was on medical leave. I began to think that if I died no one would care. I hated the fact that no one seemed to know that I would appreciate it if they came to see me. I felt empty and that feeling put me over the edge. Imagine me needing anti-depressants."

How could such a well-functioning, successful, medical icon and stable family man fall apart so dramatically? Was there something in William's history that was unearthed by his stroke? The next chapter examines William's past and the past of others and explores the dynamics that set in motion the psychological immune system and the formation and demise of the caretaker personality.

EXERCISE: BEHAVIORS TO NOTICE

1. Frequency with which I offer unsolicited advice.
2. Actions I take that are associated with guilt.
3. My real versus pretend interactions with friends, family and intimates.
4. People that are irritated by my giving who seem to avoid me.
5. Appearance of self-sufficiency as though I don't need anything.
6. Rarity of times that I disagree with anyone, or show anger, disappointment or hurt.
7. Avoidance of confrontation and conflict at all times.

6

PRIMED TO PLEASE

I have rarely encountered symptoms of caretaker disorder and the addiction to please that originated in adult life. When it has occurred, the denial of self-gratification was a conscious decision based on the decline or loss of a loved one, a personal tragedy such as a personal injury that rendered certain forms of gratification unlikely or a newfound religious conviction that involved celibacy and restraint of pleasure. Kathleen's daughter fell victim to cancer, for example, and vowed to spend the balance of her life devoting her time and attention to fund-raising for cancer research. In another case, Jake, a thirty-four-year-old CEO, left wealth and a successful career to lead a religious life of sexual abstinence and service to others in order not to yield to his homosexual inclinations. Kathleen and Jake sought therapy for reasons that were unrelated to care addiction. There was no history of early trauma in either case. Almost every case of caretaker addiction that

I have treated involved a toxic family history with one or more traumatic events. These events are recalled in various stages of therapy and in varying degrees that include flash memories, dreams, partial recall or, in time, total recall and the reexperiencing of emotion related to the traumatic event.

BRIEF HISTORIES

The notion that a childhood event can shape the adult personality evokes a range of reactions. When I was in graduate school my classmates and I were asked to write an opinion paper on that subject and we took turns presenting our ideas. My position on this matter since graduate school has remained as follows: that childhood events, particularly traumatic events, have a profound influence on adult development. The professor gave us the option to speak about our own childhood in support of our position. I shared the fact that my father abandoned my three siblings and me when I was four years old and how I thought that event influenced my life. One of my classmates responded to my presentation by saying that therapists always blame the parents and that the word *abandonment* was an overused cliché. He then made a personal reference to reinforce his position and said (paraphrased): "You were fortunate enough to have a wonderful replacement in your stepfather to make up for the loss, so how can you give so much weight to something that happened so long ago?" I could only defend my position by making logical connections. From what I can recall I said something like, "When he (my biological father) left, in my mind, I replaced him as the father of my siblings and that influenced my need to help others and later my decision to become a psychologist." At the time of course the concept of caretaker did not exist and I certainly had a limited understanding of psychological trauma. The professor then asked the class a question that I thought supported my classmate's position: "When we do make such past-present connections how does that help the patient?" The same classmate responded, "It is of limited value. Why go through the basement when you can go through the front door?" All eyes gazed in my direction waiting for my response, as I paused before responding: "Maybe by helping the patient embrace rather than erase the past he or she can get past it."

Today, I would modify my response in this fashion: With the help of the therapist patients begin to realize that the danger he or she once feared was real then, but does not exist to the same degree in the present. The specific "danger" that jump-started the immune system into action and in effect created the caretaker personality is highlighted in this chapter.

FEELING INVISIBLE: THE TRAUMA OF NOT BEING NOTICED

The feelings a human being experiences when being ignored probably range from being annoyed to being terrified. Now, I would be upset if no one read this book and I would be gravely disappointed if my publisher read it and changed every word. However, if someone in my personal life whom I was supposedly close to and who I assumed loved me treated me as though I wasn't even there, I would be devastated! Imagine how a child is impacted when his or her environment is nonresponsive or responsive in a nonnurturing, neglectful or abusive manner.

The factor most often related to the development of the addiction to please is early-childhood trauma associated with feelings of being ignored, rejected or abandoned by a primary caregiver. The indelible impression made upon the developing child is difficult to overestimate, especially when the faulty interaction with a caregiver is experienced as *traumatic*. The shock experience is instinctively generalized from the caregiver to all others, at least the majority of the time. In effect, the unconscious "believes" that everyone and anyone is a potential agent of psychological and emotional harm. In an effort to avoid the memories and suffering of the past the true, spontaneous self is "buried" and the caretaker lifestyle, the consistent and persistent focus on others, is "born." By midlife this diversion (from self and pain) has become a perversion and living for others has become an addiction!

In addition to the above, there are a variety of secondary factors that lead to compulsive pleasing behaviors that include birth order (firstborn a candidate), identification with a parent who is by definition a caretaker, or, the opposite, becoming a pleaser because a parent is narcissistic and self-absorbed (counteridentification). Extreme religious teachings that require giving to others as an exclusive mode of functioning, a distortion of the golden rule (treat others only as you would have them treat you) and complex environmental and biological factors are other possibilities.

THE NATURE OF PSYCHOLOGICAL TRAUMA

In simple terms, psychological trauma is an assault on an individual that shocks and freezes the ability to function. This overwhelming experience renders it impossible for its victim (especially a child, of course) to understand and articulate what is happening at the time of its occurrence. The memory of the traumatic event and the emotions associated with it are frozen in time and the affected individual proceeds with life as if the event never occurred. The psychological immune system in tandem with the biological immune system has done its job and life goes on. Examples of traumatic events include mental and emotional abuse, divorce, loss of a parent, sibling or close friend, exposure to assault or death, hostage or holocaust experiences, incest, rape or molestation, health threats, loss of limb, accidents, retirement, the threat of incarceration or the reality of financial ruin.

CHAPTER 6

SCENARIOS SPECIFICALLY LEADING TO THE ADDICTION TO PLEASE

Abandonment

To understand the impact of abandonment on the impressionable child I believe it's important to describe the normal process of *separation.* By separation I mean the developmental ongoing process that allows individuals to become self-directed and self-defined in a manner that is distinct from their early parental and familial influences. The degree of separation from these influences is dependent upon many factors, not the least of which is a consistent, stable family environment. This notion underscores the intent and desire most parents have for their children to provide a healthy environment that leads to optimal independent living in the future. The forward movement of the separation process, without disruption, is to a great extent dependent upon the role of the primary caregiver as an impediment or facilitator. Separation is a desirable, wholesome, interdependent dynamic that takes place throughout the life cycle. The family is in a position to facilitate this process. Abandonment is an undesirable, unwholesome, unilateral arbitrary act that is imposed on a passive recipient–and is anything but a mutual, collaborative investment. Under these circumstances the early family environment has the power to derail separation and freeze part of the individual's psychological development.

For caretakers abandonment trauma usually results in hypervigilance and hypersensitivity with regard to the presence of others. Caretakers are consumed with thoughts about what others are thinking. Owing to their toxic history they are obsessed with the feeling that people are always thinking about them and presume that those thought are always negative. These thoughts are of course unconscious, a state that accounts for their unyielding power and influence on the caretaker's lifestyle. Other mental illnesses that create distance in relationships are primarily concerned with fears of engulfment or being devoured, or fears of being destroyed, persecuted or annihilated. Caretakers are likewise affected by such fears but they are much more phobic with regard to feeling alone, unloved and invisible. Not surprising, for the caretaker, contact at any price–even abuse–is better than no contact at all. In addition, the fear of abandonment can be just as debilitating for the pleaser as actual abandonment. The emotions associated with actual or anticipated physical abandonment include guilt, resentment, rage, hate, depression, panic, helplessness, anxiety, emptiness, psychosomatic reactions, envy and deprivation–the emotions pleasing behavior are determined to keep out of awareness forever!

Emotional Distancing

The young child can be traumatized by abandonment even though both parents are physically present. I refer to this phenomenon as "emotional distancing." Stated another way, parents may be physically available to the child but may be emotionally unavailable to him or her. When this occurs the child experiences the same variety of emotions as if one or more parents actually were absent.

Marla was what I refer to as a "chameleon-pleaser." She was the youngest of four children and the only girl. She described her siblings and her parents as funny and sarcastic especially when she was being serious. Feeling ignored emotionally and upset about not being taken seriously, in order to be noticed Marla learned at an early age to put her feelings aside and act just like her family members. As years went by she continued the pattern in all her relationships and lost touch with her true feelings. During her initial therapy session she told me she did not know how she felt about the man she was about to marry. "I was just going along with the program. He asked me and I said okay."

The only time Michael got any reaction at all from his mother is when he would help her take care of his father who was immobilized following a car accident. He told me in session that for that reason he was glad his father was in a wheelchair. Lillian's father was an alcoholic and her mother was absorbed in a deep depression. Her only recourse to avoid feeling invisible with them and in life in general was to do everything for them that they asked and make other efforts to please them even when not asked. She said, "By managing their finances, driving them everywhere, cooking for them, buying things for them and listening to their problems, even though they didn't do much for me, got me noticed and made me feel worthy as a human being." How did she meet her basic needs for love, affection and emotional nurturance? Lillian weighed 275 pounds. Marla, Michael and Lillian were treated for caretaker personality disorder.

Sexual Trauma (Molestation, Incest and Rape)

The frozen or split-off aspect of the personality that lies beneath the surface of the caretaker is anathema to the formation of intimate adult relationships. In some cases, the impact of unresolved abandonment trauma can be minimized and meaningful attachments to others can occur. I would suggest, however, that such a result (therapeutic intervention notwithstanding) is usually the result of just plain *luck*. I have known individuals with abandonment fears rooted in childhood who were fortunate enough to meet a stable partner whom they felt secure with and lived happily ever after. For example, Jack somehow convinced his fiancée that she did not have to do anything extra for him and that he accepted her for who she was. His repeated efforts to assure her that her caretaking was not necessary led to a balance of give and receive and the relationship flourished. For reasons that probably invite extensive research I have found that such a fortuitous occurrence is less likely when the pleaser is masking a sexual trauma. Sexually traumatized please addicts are prone to make problematic relationship choices from the beginning of their contact with a prospective partner. When I make this observation in session the response is usually, "I don't go out looking for the wrong person." My reply is usually akin to "it's like seeing a red light and going through it knowing there are consequences." As the relationship takes shape the toxic past contaminates the interaction between the two and the future of the relationship is doomed. Mistrust and suspicion rule the day. Encounters are often sexually, rather than emotionally based, promiscuity may be rampant, and prostitution (pleasing others for a fee) is not out of the question. The victim may seek dependent partners in order to maintain control and power and avoid the helplessness and submission they felt as a child. However, they allow themselves to be gratified only within a context that insures their safety from retrauma.

When Evelyn was nine years old she recalls that her father would enter her room when her mother was asleep and "play" with her under the covers. He was a busy financial executive on Wall Street in New York City and according to Evelyn, "when he was around it was like a holiday and I would do anything to please him." She came to therapy in order to put an end to her pattern of submitting to older men, sexually and in other ways. "I felt I was in love with my boyfriend Joey, but would constantly cheat on him with much older men. I told him about the cheating and he still stuck by me because I said I would go for help. When I asked him to beat me before we had sex he broke up with me." Evelyn was confused because the men she had sex with thrived on her being pleasing and submissive. She related that her boyfriend wanted to give her "normal" love and that she couldn't receive it comfortably.

I have encountered very few cases of please addiction wherein childhood trauma was not part of the addict's history. One such case is the patient in a midlife crisis that diverted attention from his suffering quite by accident by becoming over-involved with helping others. He was out of work and took a position as a volunteer in a nursing home—and got "hooked" on pleasing. This is similar to the drug addict with no history of trauma who began an addiction after experimenting with drugs. Another example of nontrauma please addiction is the case of a female from a "perfect" family. The family system was void of disharmony and tension and the family members were always pleasant toward one another. The patient in this case never learned how to express anger nor deal with conflict. She became a school counselor in a position to help others with their problems; however, her lack of skill at conflict resolution and her excessively accommodating behavior prevented her from having intimate relationships. At the age of forty-six she had not been a relationship for more than nine months. In her case, the absence of trauma and pleasing lead to a life of emptiness.

Thus far I have discussed selflessness as an addiction, the power of the unconscious that manifests in compulsive pleasing behavior, the ultimate failure of the immune system that featured the mask of kindness (at first, we love them and then we get rid of them), the historical factors that lead to a lifestyle of deprivation and emptiness and the severe consequences that can prevail when the immune system falls apart that include suicide. In spite of these dangers, please addicts resist change—the primary focus of chapter 7.

TRAUMA DETECTION

For a minimum of one week for several hours per day focus your full attention on your childhood experiences, particularly those which you remember as negative, involving your primary caregivers. You are likely to experience memory traces after several days. In addition, during that week write down any dreams or fantasies you may have that may be related to childhood experiences. If you meet the criteria of "caretaker" as defined in this book and if you scored in the moderate or severe category on the Selfless Personality Scale, review your biography with an experienced psychotherapist. If you already know you had a psychological trauma in your past and you have not been in psychotherapy because you seem to be functioning okay or better, you may wish to see an experienced therapist for a consultation.

7

THE PURSUIT OF THE LOST SELF

One of the joys that many of us experience while being around children is observing and listening to their unabashed, unadulterated honesty. When I reflect upon that I think about their spontaneity and unharnessed, unedited expressions. The very young child is a bundle of impulses just firing away and not particularly concerned about who is listening or watching. Children are not mature enough to worry about convention or the norms of society. Unless wearing a costume for Halloween or deliberately playing a game, children simply act naturally; one might say they are maskless. With the passage of time it becomes necessary to make behavioral modifications and adapt to others in an environment that has become increasingly interpersonal. However, when the self was damaged by a trauma experience, reflexively and without planning, the true self is transformed into a false self. The spontaneity and free-spirited nature of childhood is compromised far beyond that which convention requires and replaced by a coping strategy devised by the psychological immune system. The resultant relentless other-focus and the absence of self-focus however leave wounded children in a state of emotional fragmentation and interpersonal obscurity. Their legacy is that they are remembered for what they did ("annoy people with their kindness") and not for who they are. To begin to change, caretakers need to learn that they can receive attention and genuine caring by acting naturally without having to prove their worth on a daily basis. They also need to trust that in doing so they will not be converted into being viewed as a selfish bastard.

GEOMETRY 101

The reconnection to the true self begins with what I refer to as a "geometric reconfiguration." This initial phase of recovery (transition) is a daunting task primarily because the anxiety that was erased by selflessness needs to be embraced, a process that requires a great deal of support and a spiritual conviction that includes the hope that change is possible. This challenge is discussed further in subsequent chapters. The first task of the reconfiguration is to reverse the figure-ground relationship between the self and others by making the self the figure and the other the background. Another way of stating this is the caretaker is committed to shift other-focus to self-focus. Caution: that is not a design for selfishness even though that is usually the caretaker's initial reaction. The second related task is to begin to establish horizontal rather than vertical relationships with other people. Again, the capacity to do this requires considerable anxiety reduction. The third task involved in the pursuit of the true self is more complex and involves the reduction of guilt. Here's a summary of this stage of transition.

1. Reverse figure-ground in all relationships shifting attention primarily to self while considering others as usual.
2. Reconfigure vertical-horizontal position in all relationships creating mutuality, reciprocity and balance in give-receive.
3. Recognize guilt as substitute for anxiety and increase anxiety tolerance.

The caretakers accustomed to "inventing" distractions and diversions from the powerful toxic effects of trauma, conveniently turn to guilt when someone they care about is in need or troubled. Guilt reinforces the figure-ground relationship ("they are important, not me") and the vertical position ("they need me; I don't need them"). The case of Gabriella illustrates this point.

She stated in session, "How can I go on living when my daughter is in jail? If my daughter is trapped in prison I should be in there with her," as if there is no space in the universe for Gabriella and her daughter's plight to coexist and a gross figure-ground distortion. She is also assuming that she has some control over her daughter and the legal system as if she is "above it all." This grandiosity and delusion of self-importance reinforces her vertical position and serves as a distraction from Gabriella's empty existence. The guilt-laden mother had not considered the possibility that she does not have to give up her existence and be in the same "space" as her daughter in order to be caring and supportive. These three tasks (1–3 above) are possible to accomplish when the guilt (anxiety) has diminished to the extent that the addict, in collaboration with his or her support system, is prepared to begin to pursue the journey of self-focus.

This scenario does not come about that easily. The perennial helpers have been accustomed to operating from a position of strength, if not superiority. It is they who have always been in control of their relationships . . . they have always had the answers . . . others need them, etc. For these and a myriad of reasons many please addicts and the helping professionals among them do not seek help. *When the immune system has been so effective in masking trauma, the helper is oblivious to the possibility that he or she is in danger of falling apart.* When I made that statement to a group of doctors at a major New York hospital, it was followed by a deafening silence that one could hardly hear a stethoscope drop in the auditorium. I had noticed that in the rear, one of the doctors was standing waiting to be recognized. In a reaction to my statement he proceeded to defend the entire medical profession. He said, "We have taken an oath that our patients come first and we come second. We cannot consider anything less than complete sacrifice and dedication to them." (How vertical can one get?) Suddenly, the previously subdued audience was transformed into an atmosphere of crosstalk and controversy when another doctor stood up and offered: "My dear colleague may have missed the point of Dr. Barbanell's statement. He is saying something we all know but are reluctant to admit. We can provide a service to our patients and also have a life. In addition, we may have our own emotional issues and we can address them without compromising our commitment to others and our professional ethics."

When the unbearable consequences of the caretaker syndrome, feeling invisible, empty, unloved and abandoned, lead to the admission of powerlessness over the addiction to please the first step to recovery has been taken. This admission is similar to the first step in most rehabilitation programs. Once the helper admits to needing help and actually contacts a therapist the shift from other-focus to self-focus has begun. The geometric configurations referred to above (Figure-ground, horizontal-vertical) are now in position to be reversed. During the therapy process guilt and concern for others gradually become less prominent. As this process continues the unloved, unnourished, forever ignored, previously abandoned caretaker is in a "new" position: Someone is finally paying attention on an emotional level without the pleaser having to do anything special to earn it. Most of the energy that has been expended toward others can be used to face the past and the release of emotions that were frozen in time. There is less need to harness the anxiety and panic that is freed for expression in the safety of the office setting. It is okay to function without pretending and without a mask. It is okay to expose scars and imperfections.

Taking what others have to offer (beginning with the therapist) becomes more tolerable and even gratifying. A hidden but significant benefit of the therapeutic milieu is that the therapist and the patient are both attending to the welfare of the patient—from a historical/biographical perspective—a unique experience indeed! During this initial phase of recovery, the next step on the path to self-focus entails the administration of the "Selfless Personality Scale." The scale actually "forces" self-attentiveness with diminished anxiety and guilt. The completion of the scale provides a large "dose" of attention without the compulsion to please.

THE SELFLESS PERSONALITY SCALE

The scale consists of twenty-two statements. The subject is asked to provide the responses that best describe typical actions toward others. The responses are recorded as follows: always (5), most of the time (4), some of the time (3), rarely (2), never (1). The maximum score is 105.

1. Avoid expressing anger ___
2. Put others before myself ___
3. Prefer to listen rather than be listened to ___
4. Stay with status quo, avoid change ___
5. Uncomfortable receiving gifts, compliments ___
6. Get rejected for no apparent reason ___
7. Feel empty inside ___
8. Have opportunities for fun and pleasure ___
9. Say "yes" when intended to say "no" ___

10. Fearful others will leave me permanently ___
11. Feel guilty when enjoying myself ___
12. Outraged when I ask for something and it's refused ___
13. Perceive myself as independent and self-sufficient ___
14. Believe my problems are a burden to others ___
15. Taken for granted ___
16. People are not available when I need something ___
17. Feel selfish when I do need something especially if I do ask ___
18. Need to be needed by most people most of the time ___
19. Feel good only when I am helping others ___
20. Comply when asked for a favor ___
21. Listen to others rather than disclose anything about myself ___

Score categories are as follows:

0–20	Benign
21–40	Mild
41–60	Moderate
61–80	Serious
81–105	Severe

Scores between 61 to 105 may be considered in the category of *addiction*. Scores of 4 or 5 on items 4, 15, 16 and 18 are of critical importance irrespective of total score and may be highly correlated with caretaker personality disorder or the addiction to selflessness.

DISCUSSION

Guilt (11) neutralizes anger (1) that can evoke confrontation, aggression and conflict in relation to others. Guilt is an internal (intrapersonal) process that is experienced as emotionally safer in comparison to anger, whereas anger is an external (interpersonal) process that places the caretaker at risk for rejection and isolation. Bypassing joy and pleasure (8) (19) (11), putting others first (2), giving advice, especially unsolicited advice (12) and feeling uncomfortable receiving gifts and compliments (5) yield the deceptive appearance of independence and self-sufficiency (13). Listening to excess (21), compliance (20), substituting "yes" for "no" (9) and the belief that problems are a burden to others (14) manifest in feelings of being taken for granted (15) and feeling empty inside (7). On the rare occasion when the caretaker does ask for a favor and is denied (16) (6), outrage (12) is rooted in an unconscious sense of entitlement after having been so kind to others. Alas, the need to be needed (18) was supposed to provide a guarantee that there will always be contact with others (10).

Meredith had the look of a helper. She had a soft voice and tentativeness about her when she spoke, a barely audible quiver. Her body posture even before speaking was humble and receptive, as if she was sending the message: "Anything I could do for you?"

During her initial phase of therapy she took the scale and scored in the *severe* category. Her kindness cost her $25,000 that she loaned but never recouped from a former boyfriend. Her employer owed her $15,000 in commissions. Her ex-husband did not pay her alimony nor child support for nearly seven years. She contracted HIV from having unprotected sex with someone to get even with her current boyfriend for cheating on her. Confronting each of these people would probably have prevented these consequences.

Retaking the scale after completing the treatment section and comparing total score is one way of measuring progress with regard to establishing and maintaining self-focus. The exercises in those chapters are intended to offset the obstacles that may occur in that pursuit. The next chapter addresses the challenges that interfere with the recovery process that include giving up the "rewards" of being a caretaker and other more subtle benefits and coping with the reluctance and resistance of receivers to allow change to take place. The role of guilt remains essential during the recovery process.

8

LIFE BEYOND TRAUMA

The previous chapters illustrated how the immune system works to prevent retrauma and the horrific resurrection of the emotions associated with traumatic events. The flaws in the system and its eventual breakdown were also illustrated. If the now vulnerable and probably depressed caretaker is to survive, the immune system will need to be reconstructed and restored in a more stable manner wherein the ability to cope is not constructed in defense, but alternatively, in the *acceptance* of past traumatic experiences.

Summarily, the previous chapters identified the specific criteria for the addiction to please (diagnosis), the unique dynamics inherent in the lifestyle of the caretaker-addict, insights into the origins of its formulation and a narrative about the beginning of recovery. The understanding and insight is an initial phase in the rebuilding process for several reasons. Caretakers become aware that their lifestyle served a particular function that had as its mission the maintenance of contact with others by devoting time, attention and energy exclusively to them, while minimizing or completely disregarding their own need states. The choreographed (by the unconscious) other-focus detracted from self-focus and effectively repressed their internal chaotic world, particularly the effects of early-childhood trauma. Having that awareness prepares them for the self-reflection process that will eventually slow their accommodation reflexes and free them to consider the possibility of an improved give-receive balance. The recognition of their persona (mask) as false sets the stage for the motivation to reconnect to their true self that could lead to the meaningful connections to others they are perpetually seeking. The revelation that their relationships are vertical is a stunning insight to caretakers who firmly believed their relationships were genuine and balanced. Furthermore, these and other insights, once processed, help them distinguish between perceptions associated with their past trauma from their present reality. This distinction separates the there and then from the here and now that can offset the generalization of constantly being "threatened" that originated in childhood and remained dormant in their unconscious mind. Before the caretakers are willing to apply these insights to their lives the obstacles to change will need to be identified, diminished or removed.

THE HELPER'S RELUCTANCE TO RECEIVE HELP

Before seeking help caretakers have reaped many of the benefits from the addiction to please. Their focus on others is a source of pride that counterbalances the internal shame and guilt they are relentlessly determined to conceal. They have successfully distracted themselves from the pain of the past and remain in a safe emotional zone, temporarily shielded from the remnants of trauma. In a sense, they have achieved status among their peers and discovered that they have found a way to fit in that is ego enhancing and socially respected. They feel loved and connected even without reciprocity. Essentially, they have been living a life that assures them of ongoing contact with the human race, a life they are reluctant to change because in their reality they are thriving. For those individuals the immune system is intact and may remain in that state. For others, those who finally seek help, the benefits have begun to be outweighed by the consequences. Time has passed and they still feel unloved and emotionally disconnected from others and/or a midlife crisis has penetrated the system and reopened old wounds. The "cracks in the armor" humble the caretaker who no longer feels emotionally safe and stable.

Pleasers who begin therapy are usually reluctant participants in the process. Recall that receiving makes them uncomfortable, a state that mitigates against asking for anything from anyone. Throughout their history the possibility of exposing their vulnerable side was never a consideration. They typically seek help ostensibly because of the loss of a job, a relationship breakup, mental exhaustion, panic attacks, migraine and assorted somatic complaints, feeling trapped and overobligated, weight problems, social and emotional isolation or the realization that "something is missing." They do not suspect for a moment that their initial complaint is not the fundamental reason they are troubled and that it is their selflessness that is the primary cause of their emotional upheaval. For example, on rare occasions the prospective patient will express that she or he is angry with regard to being exploited or taken for granted, probable symptoms of caretaker disorder. Also infrequent is the complaint that "being kind has hurt me." The signs that I have observed during intake are more often related to guilt about seeking help: "I am here at a time when everyone around me needs me." In severe cases, the please addict has been recommended for therapy following one or more suicide attempts.

As the process begins, the interface between therapist and patient is extremely awkward. The figure-ground configuration is reversed. Here, the patient is in the foreground of attention and the other person, in this case the therapist, is in the background. Likewise, the vertical-horizontal positioning is reversed: the therapist is "above" and the patient is "below." The early phase of treatment then is an ongoing struggle on the part of the patient to fight off these reversals. *The primary obstacle toward recovery from the addiction to please is the caretakers themselves.* In the middle and later phases of treatment as the therapist encourages the practice of asking and receiving, their resistance is even more tangible: "Are you teaching me to be a selfish bitch?" My response is typically something like, "You may feel selfish when you say 'no' to others, but that may be because you are comparing yourself to your history of always saying 'yes'." Yes, the caretaker no longer wants to feel empty, wants more meaningful intimate attachments and is worn out from feeling obligated to everyone (obligations are a form of contact). However, the path to self-focus is never a "straight line" as addicts waver between changing their lifestyle and catering to the needs of others. This stubborn refusal to change is punctuated and perpetuated by *guilt*. Caretakers are convinced that their receivers cannot exist without them and that to stop indulging them would "ruin them and I would feel responsible." This belief is obviously grandiose and irrational and any reasonable caretaker would agree when informed. However, the power of the addiction is such that the compulsion to please will not be easily deterred.

Here is an example of resistance to change from a group therapy session:

> *Monica*: I can't keep up with everybody. I spent my entire week going to doctors for my mother. I think she's a hypochondriac. I am exhausted and I think it's my thyroid.
>
> *Group Member*: We know how busy you get taking care of everyone, and not only your mother. Do you ever ask your son to help around the house? He lives at home, doesn't he?
>
> *Monica*: He's got a drug problem and he's a mixed-up kid [age thirty-six]. He can't do anything to help me.
>
> *Group member*: I was wondering if he contributes to the rent. Is it okay that I asked you that?
>
> *Monica:* Huh! That would be amazing . . . he doesn't even do his own laundry.
>
> *Group Member*: I'm sorry, that's a joke isn't it? You allow that . . . how come?
>
> *Monica:* Who will do it if I don't? I've always done it.

Group Member: Try not doing it for one week and tell us what happens.

Monica: Oh, I don't know. I guess I can try.

Monica returned to the group the following week and reported that her son did his own laundry for the first time. She had done everything for him to make certain he would never leave her, a selfless role with a self-serving motive. A typical caretaker, Monica's history reveals that she was primed to please. At the age of five, her father died of cancer. Her mother, preoccupied with her own grief, was not attentive to Monica's suffering over the loss of her father. The mother remarried within a year. Consumed by the relationship to her second husband she continued to ignore Monica's needs for support, attention and affection, until one day her mother smiled when the then six-year-old Monica gave her a flower. Monica finally discovered a way to get attention on an emotional level from her mother. Of course, she had generalized that "successful" interaction toward others, her son being a significant beneficiary of her kindness. I gave Monica a copy of the following poem:

A Message for the Caretaker
Water flowers too much, too often, they drown and wither away.
Only when they need it, they last beyond another day.
That others can't survive . . . weak only in your eyes?
When you let go they survive, much to your surprise.
The Mask of Kindness, a cover to conceal.

Remove it and discover you shift from fake to real.
The intent was not to deceive . . . the mask was just to cope.
It's okay to receive; with self-focus there is hope.
Just like flowers, if I may mention . . . even *you* need attention!

OTHER OBSTACLES TO CHANGE AND RECOVERY

If and when the mask of kindness is removed caretakers become confused in their thoughts and tentative in their actions. Accordingly their dreams and their fantasies convey a wish to return to their former state when for them life was more predictable. The following summary statement illustrates what I consider a "doubt attack": "I have been this way my whole life. Isn't it too late to change? I wouldn't know how to act, I would lose all my friends, and my family and others who love me won't recognize me. You know what, I don't know if I would recognize me." The importance of an empathic response to such statements is critical. Caretakers in transition and en route to recovery are uncertain and anxious about what happens after the mask is removed and true feelings are exposed. They are actually contemplating changing a lifelong pattern, a courageous endeavor indeed that requires an extremely understanding, supportive environment. My typical response to a doubt attack is as follows: "Change is a process that is both frightening and exciting. We are all reluctant to give up what we know whether or not it was always beneficial and I can appreciate what you are giving up. You are not likely to suddenly cease to be thoughtful, considerate and helpful to others, but you are less likely to exclude yourself as you practice allowing others to give to you."

THE UNCOOPERATIVE ENVIRONMENT

"I've Grown Accustomed" (adapted from *My Fair Lady*)

I've grown disgusted with your face,
it makes me wish my day would end.
You're nice, you're sweet, but I must retreat.
I wish you well in your disguise
and that soon you will get wise.
I was extremely independent and
content before we met.
I choose to stay that way, you need not fret.
I've grown disgruntled with your ways,
And wish you better days.

The support that caretakers require when in transition is not always available (see retraining, chapter 9). Even caring, well-wishing family members, friends and intimates may be reluctant to give up the benefits they have been receiving. Receivers have been programmed by the givers to depend on them and as the latter relinquish their persona the transformation goes unnoticed and is initially ignored as if no change has taken place. This is dishearténing to caretakers who took the chance of doing something "out-of-the-box." The conscious or unconscious resistance on the part of others is understandable in the sense that having been indulged in the past they are now inconvenienced and have to fend for themselves. More middle-aged sons will have to do their own laundry and contribute to the rent. Husbands may have to pay for the nanny their mother-in-law stopped subsidizing. Grandchildren will have to manage with fewer gifts when grandma comes to the house. Moreover, when the caretakers begin to say "no" the displeasure of others becomes even more conspicuous. When the changes are not noticed or welcomed with enthusiasm ("They won't let me change."), caretakers cannot fathom that the fulfillment they have been seeking is ever possible. On the contrary, they begin to panic and have thoughts that the adjustments they are making may destroy their relationships and return them to the dreaded state of invisibility they spent a lifetime avoiding.

The case of Jenny illustrates the frustration and disappointment of a caretaker in transition. During her marriage of eighteen years she periodically mentioned to her husband that having a child was a priority. In spite of the fact that they had not had sex over a three-year period, his response was always affirmative. Repeatedly, she would bring up the subject and he would respond the same way—only verbally, as their sex life remained nonexistent. Jenny began to realize that she had trained her husband that her priorities, in or outside of the bedroom, were not that important. As she approached forty and became increasingly anxious and brought up the issue more often, her husband responded in predictable fashion and the subject would then be dismissed. Encouraged by the support of her therapy group and the empathy of a friend Jenny confronted her husband and told him that his "double talk" was no longer acceptable. Confronting, asking and pursuing others with regard to her needs and wishes were unique occurrences in Jenny's life. They did have sex that evening but unfortunately for Jenny in the weeks and months that followed her husband continued to be nonresponsive to sexual and other needs she had learned to convey. Although she had made progress the lack of response from her husband was reminiscent of her feelings of being emotionally ignored as a child. At the time, she hit a detour on her path to self-focus and relapsed into the guilt-caretaker mode once again. Techniques for the management of detours on the path of self-focus and exercises to facilitate the recovery from the addiction to please are presented in the next chapter.

HIGHLIGHTS

- Insight and understanding with regard to the dynamics of selflessness, including the awareness of its benefits and consequences, are a prerequisite toward recovery from the addiction to please.
- The reluctance to compromise the benefits of helping others and guilt are among the major obstacles to the alteration of the caretaker lifestyle.

- As caretakers become aware that others do not need them as much as they thought they did they are surprised that others can fend for themselves.
- During the transition phase, the lack of response from others can be offset by the determination to stay on the path to self-focus and not be discouraged or seduced by guilt.

9

THREE RS: REBUILDING, RETRAINING, RECOVERY

As discussed in chapter 8 there are a variety of obstacles in the care addict's effort to change, not the least of which is the receivers' reluctance to allow the change to take place by guilt induction and other discouraging actions they may take. During that transition period the caretaker is exposed to increasing levels of anxiety related to feeling unprotected by the psychological immune system. The system had been either totally decimated by a breakdown or, preferably, gradually dismantled with the aid of professional intervention. Presumably, the mask of kindness has either been loosened or removed. Repressed feelings continue to surface, the impact of childhood trauma is significantly reduced, and the essence of the true self begins to emerge. *The improvement in self-esteem during this period is dependent upon self-acceptance and the degree of positive reinforcement from others and is no longer reliant on the temporary emotional blind spots.* Through introspection many of the caretaker's "blind spots" are removed. The insights gained have the potential to neutralize the compulsive need to be needed and pave the way to new behaviors. Among these possibilities are a more balanced give-receive interaction with others and the capability for real, intimate connections to them. When the care addicts begin to trust that in order to be noticed they are not compelled to please, their rehabilitation becomes a realistic possibility.

REBUILDING

The reconstruction of the immune system entails the replacement of the false, accommodating persona with authentic communication and behavior without a self-serving hidden agenda. The "rebuilt" version of the protective system is less rigid and more elastic; the need to hide from the self is not as intense and urgent. Attending to the needs of others becomes a *choice*, rather than an obsession. The successful transfer of insight and understanding into behavior depends upon the repetition and follow-up of noncaretaking behavior. For example, asking for something needs to be repeated over time for others to notice the shift. People who have grown accustomed to not being asked will require more frequent repetitions than others. Considering the life span of the caretaker's former protective maneuvers this rebuilding stage is facillitated by a variety of exercises and interventions.

The Hidden Contract

Caretakers have an unwritten contract in their mind that no one knows about. Its power lies in the fact that the contract is hidden in the "drawer" of the unconscious mind. When potential receivers feel pressure to comply with the "agreement" they usually do not cooperate. The offended caretaker in response to the rejection feels hurt and angry (see box 9.1).

At the base of the contract is a space for two signatures. The caretaker has virtually signed in both spaces. The other party (almost everyone he or she encounters in life) is not in on the agreement but is somehow expected to comply. (The contract is another testament to the ingenuity of the psychological immune system.)

A visual representation of the contract and its implications makes it easier for caretakers to alter their behavior by adjusting their unrealistic expectations and better manage their sense of entitlement. In the best-case scenario, in a symbolic way, they are in a better position to "tear up" the guarantee that was created to insure an end to their loneliness. In the group therapy example below, note the unstated expectations of the pleaser and the reaction from an oblivious (to the agreement) noncompliant group member.

A group member disgusted with the caretaker's ongoing attention-seeking efforts to please the group reacted by ignoring her for a month. When the issue was brought out in the open the frustrated group member related: "Week after week in group I felt like I was in elementary

BOX 9.1
SAMPLE CARETAKER CONTRACT

I (name of caretaker), agree to the following:

(a) I will comply with your wishes and requests whether or not they are an inconvenience to me.
(b) I will place your needs ahead of mine at all times.
(c) I shall avoid confronting you even when you displease me. You will never be victimized by my anger.
(d) You will always and forever trust my reliability and loyalty.

In return for my uncompromising dedication to you, as stipulated above, you agree to never leave me or ignore me and you will accept me at all times.

Signature______________________________

____

Signature______________________________

____

school playing 'show-and-tell.' The other kids would bring in anything they wanted and I had to watch and act interested. I must have been in third grade when one day a kid brought in shoelaces, a bottle of his father's hair tonic and a White Castle hamburger that was half-eaten and probably a week old. When the kid did five minutes on the shoelaces I fell asleep. I got suspended because the teacher thought I was faking it and mocking the kid's presentation . . . smart teacher." The frustrated group member's message was: "Stop controlling me by assuming everything you offer is of interest to me."

The Obligation Checklist

The accumulations of obligations that are both self-generated and imposed by others fill the daily planner of caretaker personalities. Guilt is the intractible force and the key ingredient that maintains the length of the list of obligations. The preparation of the list calls to the caretakers' attention that their routine obligations are succeeding in diverting them not only from their desire for joy, pleasure, love and meaningful relationships, but also from the relief of their suffering. The list is constructed by drawing a line down the center of a page (box 9.2). On one side of the page is written, "Things I Did–and Didn't Want to Do." On the other side is written, "Things I Want to Do–and Did." The contents of the list include actions taken during a period of two weeks or more. The items are those that are significant such as driving a friend somewhere after working a ten-hour day, or giving a friend the balance in your checkbook and neglecting to pay the rent, and so on. The "Want to . . . " side is invariably much shorter and typically contains no more than five items.

The act of making the comparison and having this visual "snapshot" at hand alerts the caretakers to a major cause

BOX 9.2
SAMPLE OBLIGATION CHECKLIST

Things I Did—And Didn't Want To
1. Get involved in my son's drug problems.
2. Make my boss's personal calls.
3. Make sure everyone is having a good time.
4. Act as if I adore my mother-in-law.
5. Pay my brother's rent.
6. Give my daughter money for breast implants.
7. Take a friend to the airport on my only day off.

Things I Want to Do—And Did
1. Had a slice of Sicilian pizza.
2. Read a book.
3. Played chess.

of their fatigue, anxiety and depression. Moreover, they are able to "see" why they feel unfulfilled, overwhelmed and trapped by their overresponsible nature. The checklist is but one technique intended to help caretakers learn to say "no" and allow others to become less reliant upon them. As their obligation list becomes more balanced, the thought of depression or suicide as "the only way out" of the obligation trap becomes increasingly remote.

The Give-Receive Chart

This exercise highlights the give-receive imbalance that helps the caretaker maintain a delusional sense of superiority, control and independence. The additional downside, of course, is that most if not all of their relationships are superficial and fake (since meaningful, genuine relationships require a give-receive balance) The instructions are the same as with the "Obligation Checklist" except that on

BOX 9.3
SAMPLE GIVE-RECEIVE CHART

Acts of Giving (one-week duration)

1. Visitors never left empty-handed.
2. Paid wealthy daughter's mortgage.
3. Worked a double shift without compensation.
4. Cleaned my son's room and did his laundry after bailing him out of jail for a drug bust.
5. Visited a friend in the hospital four times this week.
6. Cancelled a concert to drive a friend to the airport.
7. Made my boss's personal phone calls and picked up his dry cleaning.
8. Attended the wedding of a coworker and bought her an expensive gift because I thought she would appreciate it.

Acts of Receiving (same week)

1. Had sex this week.
2. Went for coffee with a friend.
3. Accepted a compliment.

this chart the division is between "Giving Behavior" and "Receiving Behavior." Again, the disparity between both lists is usually conspicuous, particularly because pleasers are so uncomfortable with receiving.

The Path to Self-Focus

As discussed in previous chapters the lifestyle of someone with a caretaker personality disorder, of those addicted to please, is a safe road in the near term that at a later stage is morphed into a road to ruination. The ubiquitous and relentless concentration of effort and time invested in others has been reinforced by guilt that is equally ubiquitous and relentless. The attempts to shift to self-focus are continually disrupted by the conscious experience of guilt and underlying anxiety. To offset the powerful effects of the guilt/anxiety dynamic the following exercise is recommended.

On the blank page of a notebook draw an actual path or road. If only for effect, make it a winding path. On each side of the path leave space for notes. (On the top of each page leave a space to indicate the date the path is created.) On each side of the path indicate all incidents that could have induced a guilty response. Below the path indicate the action taken after the guilt-induction event. Keep a tally on the number of times the event had little or no impact versus the number of times the pressure of guilt induction wins out. Do this exercise for no less than two weeks.

Here are samples from one patient's "path":

1. Bothered me that sister and brother were not speaking. Arranged a meeting between them.

2. Boss said he needed me and that I should cancel vacation plans.
3. Wife asked me to accompany her to nursing home to visit mother for ninth consecutive week.
4. Friend approached me to lend him $10,000.
5. Son let me know he wanted a new car.
6. Daughter knew I had tickets to basketball game, assumed I would babysit same night.
7. Mother (hypochondriac) got angry when I refused to take her to doctor again.

PROFESSIONAL INTERVENTION

The rebuilding of the true self requires a successful treatment plan that includes insight, understanding, catharsis, support from others, conflict and trauma resolution, conquest of guilt and guilt induction, comfort with receiving, diminished repression and increased expression of emotion, education on the power of "no" and sensitization of others to changes via repetition and follow-up in an ongoing effort to be noticed in a different manner than in the past. Although other orientations may yield positive treatment outcomes, relational analysis (RA) is a particularly effective intervention with issues related to caretaker syndrome. This view is based on the premise that emotional illness in general is the consequence of faulty relationships, especially attachments to primary caregivers that are formed early in the developmental life cycle. Accordingly, a corrective, reparative relationship with a therapist experienced in RA is the essential ingredient in the change process. An emotionally safe, trusting environment is cocreated by the mutual efforts of therapist and patient. The relationship established is horizontal rather than vertical (opposite from parent-child paradigm) and mutual rather than unilateral. In most cases a successful treatment outcome will depend upon the therapist's authenticity, self-disclosure and empathy and the patient's comfort with the *real* person of the therapist. I often recommend group therapy as an adjunct to individual treatment.

GROUP PSYCHOTHERAPY

The Essence of the Therapy Group

Few are blessed it seems with two nurturing parents.
Others less fortunate have had one attentive parent, a parent who was neglectful or abusive or no parents at all.
With boundless determination some may survive these obstacles on their own.
We know however that burden is less daunting with help along the way, from a second family . . . a group.
The hovering attention, genuine feedback and unconditional acceptance form a bond of trust and intimacy.
Together the members embrace the ongoing cycles of hope.
The group is a place to go when all seems lost.
It is here in the safest of all places that new attachments replace the impact of the toxic past. It is here that all pretense and masks are removed, the true self can reemerge, and in time, a spirit of change can prevail.

The themes addressed in individual therapy are recapitulated with the therapist during the preparation for group. Caretakers are now ready to be released from the clutches of guilt and the group support helps embrace the anxiety that had been camouflaged by guilt. The unmasked, more self-focused group member, for the very first time, has the opportunity to learn how to *ask and receive without fear*. In the months and years ahead participation affords caretakers with opportunities to practice saying "no" at nearly every meeting. The tolerance for feedback from members, including compliments, praise and even criticism, improves the previously lopsided give-receive balance. Interactions with members that allow the caretaker to express anger increase the likelihood that their relationships outside the group will be more genuine and intimate.

In addition to group, another adjunct to individual therapy is the introduction of antidepressants and/or anti-anxiety medication. The inclusion of medication in treatment planning is based on the state of the patient and the therapist's clinical judgment and expertise. Certainly when patients are in the throngs of anxiety and/or panic attacks psychotropic drugs can be helpful. Or, when the overwhelmed patient succumbs to depression, antidepressants may serve as a temporary crutch that enables the giver to function on a daily basis. The downside to medication intervention with caretakers, in my view, is that the person with a care addiction is already hooked on "drugs" (giving, accommodating, obligations, etc.) that have aided and abetted the numbing of their emotions, sexual expression and the pursuit of pleasure in general. Psychotherapy is designed to promote more and not less emotional and sexual expression and increase experiences of joy and pleasure. In that sense, "people medicine" (group therapy, self-help groups, family, friends, community), depending upon the individual case, is more often the preferred mode of intervention to psychotropic drugs.

The aura of the rebuilding phase is encapsulated in Donald's dream.

A rescue helicopter was hovering over the ocean and dropped a ladder to a man floating in the water wearing a life jacket. His boat had capsized and he was in danger of drowning. The man climbed to the middle of the ladder and spread his legs apart like someone would a chicken wing at a dinner party. One of his legs clung to the ladder and the other leg stretched out a distance to touch the side of an old, dilapidated building.

Donald was comforted by the (symbolic) option to go back to his former lifestyle of fixer, advisor, and savior . . . the "old, dilapidated building" while his emotional development was moving forward.

The rebuilding phase is characterized by seemingly endless cycles of hope and despair. The pleaser alternates between being encouraged and feeling totally defeated. In this state the therapy group and other supports serve a function similar to Alcoholics Anonymous and other self-help agencies. Support, practice, follow-up, the belief that receiving is acceptable and resilience in response to an unyielding environment are the essential ingredients in relapse prevention—especially when guilt, the internal-eternal saboteur, lies in waiting. In order for the rebuilding process to progress the determination of the caretaker to stay on the path of self-focus will be constantly tested. The moment the pleasers stop pleasing and begin to notice the reactions from those conditioned to receive from them, their guilt button is sensitized and ready to eliminate any possibility for joy and pleasure. *Recovery is contingent upon the caretakers' tolerance for setbacks and the self-blame they may inflict along the way.*

Katherine seemed to overcome her dual addiction to food and to giving, both of which were psychologically and emotionally intertwined. Her early abandonment trauma lead to the formation of the mask of kindness and the maintenance of a safe distance from others that she required in order to avoid the risk of retrauma. She substituted food for people and at the age of thirty-two she was obese. A variety of interventions helped her and she began to rebuild her life. She had a gastric bypass operation, lowered her food intake, increased her number of therapy sessions and went on a "people diet" that included less pleasing and more receiving. Several years after maintaining her weight loss and a brief time after she stopped therapy, Katherine began dating for the first time in eight years. "For the first time in my life I was in a really close relationship when my fiancé was in a car accident that changed everything." He had become dependent upon Katherine and both her addictions took hold once again. She returned to therapy and the next of the rebuilding process.

CHAPTER 9

RETRAINING (OF OTHERS)

I have not kept my fascination with unconscious processes a secret to my readers, my colleagues or my patients. There is another aspect of human behavior that I find equally compelling, that is, the frequency with which people predict other people's behavior. Both consciously and unconsciously care addicts elevate predicting behavior to an art form. Their focus on others and their underlying anxiety with regard to being accepted keep them in a state of constantly thinking about what others are thinking and how they will respond; moreover, their predictions are usually negative. In order to retrain the environment to cooperate with rebuilding a more balanced lifestyle, caretakers need to reduce their preoccupation with the future. To return to the case of Jenny in chapter 8, she constantly anticipated that her husband would ignore her wishes to get pregnant. Her anticipation inhibited her from being more forthright about her wishes. Her husband "knew" he could pacify her because she taught him that he could. The key to influencing others to cooperate is to avoid transforming what should be a dialogue into an internal monologue. For example, Jenny would have a conversation in her mind with her husband that in effect would predict the outcome: "If I tell him what I want he will act as if he heard me but the results will be the same." As a result of this prediction Jenny would refrain from the conversation because she already had the answer. When caretakers have become more tolerant of their anxiety and begin to engage others more often (switch internal monologue into a dialogue) their path to self-focus contains fewer detours.

> *Jenny*: When he does his pacifying thing lately I don't let him off the hook like I used to. I get angry and tell him over and over how important it is to me, whatever it is. It could be paying my mother a visit on a Sunday or having a baby. Maybe he gets it now!
>
> *Me*: It's always gratifying when others respond to you in a favorable way.
>
> *Jenny*: But what if I continue to be ignored? At least when I did my please thing I knew people were attentive.

The question Jenny asked about "What if . . . ?" is quite common during the retraining phase and is related to the future orientation that anxiety creates. Caretakers are faced with the challenge of breaking an interpersonal pattern that they themselves have choreographed. For them to break the pattern and reshape their relationships the following actions are helpful:

1. The conversion of internal monologues into actual dialogues regarding needs, wishes and desires by ceasing and desisting from predicting the reactions of others. (Incidentally, those predictions may be incorrect.)
2. Repetition and follow-up, with extreme patience, realizing that the creation of "this unresponsive monster" was a collaborative effort.

3. Taking the position that the *potential for reshaping* has been set in motion by open, direct dialogue irrespective of the nature of the responses from others.

As the power of the addiction to please begins to diminish the capacity to ask for more, more often, expands. Caretakers having loosened their mask feel less protected and more exposed emotionally. When the wished-for responses are not immediately forthcoming they tend to get discouraged and can easily relapse. The "new people" in their lives, less conditioned, seem to notice the changes quicker. The people who know the caretaker the longest may be the last to notice their efforts to be different. How ironic those closest to them have the ability to disrupt and derail this stage of rebuilding. Retraining others is a difficult endeavor that may not succeed in all situations. To repeat once again: *caretakers need to stay on the path to self-focus irrespective of the response they receive from others.*

RECOVERY

Recovery from the addiction to please is contingent upon the changes that take place during the rebuilding and retraining phases. Indications of improvement are that the trait, selflessness, is less prominent (less "foreground"), that a give-receive balance is more prevalent, that relationships are more "horizontal" (mutual, reciprocal) and that daily routines are not "overweighted" with obligations. When these and other improvements are in evidence the caretaker begins to experience increasing joy, pleasure, personal enrichment and true intimacy. The Selfless Personality Scale was originally proposed as a diagnostic instrument and as a tool that aids self-focus during the initial stages of psychotherapy. During the recovery stage the scale can be retaken and viewed as an objective measure of where the caretaker "is at" relative to the change process and also as an indicator of issues requiring additional attention.

KEY QUESTIONS

- What is the relationship between guilt and anxiety?
- Why is guilt the Achilles heel of change for the caretaker?
- What is the significance of the give-receive imbalance?
- How can the caretaker avoid the guilt-induction trap?
- What are some of the ways group therapy can help the caretaker attain self-focus?
- What is the downside to medication for please addicts?

10

ONCE A PLEASE ADDICT, ALWAYS A PLEASE ADDICT?

During discussions among mental health professionals at universities, training centers, workshops and seminars the subject of "cure" may be even more controversial than "unconscious." With regard to addictions specifically, cure is usually discussed in a spirit of guarded optimism bordering on skepticism. My position with regard to trait addictions is that complete cure is an ambitious but not an unattainable goal. Many caretakers often share their doubts that "it's too late . . . I have been this way my whole life." Others are apprehensive that they will become selfish or even narcissistic: "I don't want to trade one illness for another." Some are discouraged after years of progress when the environment refuses to cooperate.

The impulse to please and the guilt reflexes that reinforce the mask of kindness may not completely disappear. However, when the posttrauma psychological immune system is reconstructed and rebuilding, retraining and recovery are moving forward, the automatic accommodating behavior decreases in frequency and intensity. Put simply, the guilt reflexes begin to lose their "charge" and are held in check more often.

At the age of fifty, Nancy's caretaker lifestyle was yielding diminishing returns. She described herself as "running, running, running on empty and going nowhere." She believed her existence was a complete waste. Throughout the course of her life she had traded one addiction for another that included food, shopping, alcohol, drugs and giving to others. In her relentless determination to overcome her latent childhood fear of feeling and remaining invisible, the addiction to please was her last resort. Her treatment included individual and group psychotherapy, a gastric bypass operation, attendance at AA meetings and sessions with an allergist and nutritionist. Her recovery, in her words, "was astonishing." Her husband, children and friends were noticing the changes and responding. She became more comfortable receiving gifts and compliments and her sex life improved. She maintained her weight loss and became more productive at work. Although her confidence was growing that she had overcome most of her addictions Nancy would periodically test out her belief that she was changing because she was aware of her tendency to fool herself. She decided to go shopping and while in a department store tripped on an escalator. Her injuries left her with a fractured ankle and bruises on her forehead. She wore a support stocking that covered the cast on her ankle and wore her hair to cover the bruises on her forehead.

As she sat in her living room one day after the injury reading a book her daughter asked her to drive her to a friend's house, her son impatiently asked her for money for a haircut and her husband screamed at her for not doing his laundry. When her daughter asked that she walk the dog as she prepared for her visit to her friend, Nancy restrained herself from having a tantrum. Instead she put a barrette in her hair to expose the bruises, removed the stocking from her leg and placed her damaged ankle on the hassock in front of her hoping everyone present would get the message. The family members had been well trained by Nancy and at least for that day they had forgotten she was not the "old Nancy." What Nancy needed to relearn was that she cannot expect others to read her mind and always know what she needed—a standard she had developed for herself. *During recovery caretakers need to continue to be direct in asking to have their needs met and not expect others to be as tuned-into their needs as they had been.*

An experience I had during my own recovery from a history of pleasing others illustrates the forward-backward nature of recovery and how the change process itself is rarely linear.

Danny was born and raised in Africa. He spoke several languages but had extreme difficulty learning English. At the time I first met him he had been in this country less than ten years. His father, an engineer, had come here because of a job opportunity that eventually ended with his being fired. The family was in dire straits financially. Danny desperately wanted to help but could not find a job because of his language-related difficulties. During breaks in my schedule I would go to a local coffee shop where I would see Danny almost daily with his computer in front of him. Someone told him I was a psychologist and he approached me to tell me that if I ever needed computer assistance he was available. During the conversation I noticed that his English was very good. I could not understand why he could not find a job until he told me that his writting skills were lacking, he didn't think he could complete a resume, and he lacked confidence on an interview. I had the impression that he was not lacking the ambition or the energy to further his education and pursue a career. Both his parents were working at modest positions and loans were available. (I remain puzzled why his parents were refusing to help him.)

I was writing my first book and although I saved the contents in my computer, the computer crashed and I feared I lost everything. I returned to the store where I purchased the computer, but the technician could not diagnose the problem. In desperation I turned to Danny for help and he fixed the problem. As he was making the repair I was impressed with his technical skill and I became even more perplexed why he wasn't employed. When I offered to pay him he refused to accept the offer but conceded to letting me buy him dinner. I told him how much I appreciated his services and he replied by asking me to refer other businesspeople to him. Suddenly, my caretaking reflexes were reactivated. Dinner did not satisfy my urge to show the degree of appreciation that I was feeling.

Sparked by the skill he displayed while repairing my computer and impressed by the conversation we had during dinner, I thought of sending Danny to a colleague for intelligence testing. I followed my thought with action and suggested that he take the Wechsler Intelligence Scale for Adults. He did not know that I paid for the examination. He scored in the high average category (90–110 is average), and we discussed his intellectual strengths and weaknesses. My next move was to locate a learning center that would help him improve his language skills. I was successful in finding the center and told Danny about the program and offered to pay the tuition. When we parted company I realized that my gratitude had gone too far and left my judgment in its wake. Was I encouraging Danny to be dependent on me? Was I flaunting my superiority and expertise? Were my actions and his passive acceptance of them making it easier for Danny to coast through life and therefore ultimately harmful to him? Was it too late for damage control?

I called Danny and we set a time to meet. I told him that I was glad to have him tested and that I thought the program at the learning center would help him. I then told him I made a mistake by offering to pay the tuition and I apologized. I explained why that "extra step" would not be helpful to him. I suggested that he find a job doing almost anything that would provide income to pay for the tuition at the learning center and further that he ask his parents for assistance. He was receptive and agreed to act on my suggestions.

My experience with Danny helped me revisit and reframe my position with regard to the cure of the addiction to please, a posture I do not hesitate to discuss with my patients and the audiences at my lectures. For the caretaker the path of self-focus will always include detours. With the passage of time, however, and the slowdown of the guilt reflex there are likely to be fewer detours with less potency attached to them.

WHEN THE PARTS OF THE SELF ARE REUNITED

According to *Webster's New World Dictionary* one definition of *harmony* is "cohesive arrangements of parts." In psychology we use terms like *equilibrium*, *balance* or *homeostasis* to describe a similar state of a desired human condition and spirit. For caretakers, this condition entails the integration of selflessness into the whole personality made possible by the reconciliation of trauma experiences, embracing the emotions associated with traumatic events, being released from the shackles of guilt and the reconnecting with the true self.

NEW BEGINNINGS

Gabriella always made certain her houseguests were enjoying themselves at her home during her Christmas parties. The responsibility for their comfort diverted her from the sadness she felt around the holidays. During her recovery she was able to work through her sadness by "feeling it." At subsequent parties she was less concerned with the comfort of her guests and just enjoyed their company. "I guess I'm not Santa Claus after all."

Paula lost thirty-five pounds, began taking yoga classes, enrolled in poetry classes and learned to speak Spanish. When her friends asked her how she managed to accomplish so much in less than one year she said, "I stopped living just for my kids."

Ben's recovery was highlighted by insight and the sudden realization that running his family business was not his only purpose in life. At age forty-seven Ben became involved in a *real* intimate relationship for the first time.

Caretaker personalities like Gabriella, Paula and Ben have many things in common. They are on the path to self-focus that began with self-deception that is now leading to a more balanced lifestyle. They have traveled the distance from someday fantasies ("It's okay, in five years when I finish working . . . ."), to living for today with opportunities for greater satisfaction, fulfillment and inner peace.

"Just Me"

Once upon a time I was the true me
The me they could not see.
Looking for love I would roam,
While pleasing I found a home.
Years went by; it didn't last . . .
Too much damage from the past.
Again rejection? Too much to take.
Better off remaining fake.
Now the lessons I have learned can set me free.
Free to be loved, just being me!

EPILOGUE

Let's Get Real

The re-examination of the "lessons of life" that we have somehow inhaled can lead to interesting and important discoveries. The notion that it is not *always* better to give than to receive, for example, may be a revelation to some and may be offensive to others. An alternative of perceiving *kindness* can also have some benefits that can lead to a better quality of life. One can be kind and self-gratifying in the same lifetime. *Openness* and *honesty* are considered virtuous, but both are not *always* desirable. The statement, "I don't think there's chemistry between us" is certainly less hurtful than, "I have to tell you I think you're ugly." The latter statement is certainly more open, honest, and direct.

Romance is another concept that gets high grades by individuals in the state of falling in love. Certainly for romantics of all ages, flowers, music, poetry, fine wine and ambiance make for good times and blissful feelings. However, romance and falling in love are hardly the same. Even Freud said that falling in love and being in love are very different. It is remarkable how many intelligent, stable people make major decisions (various forms of commitment) during the romantic phase of a relationship. The violins are playing, dinner is the best, the sex is outstanding, and everyone including family and friends is "wonderful." The two lovers respect each other's space and seem to enjoy each other's hobbies and interests. Woops! They know each other less than six months. Do they really know each other, or are they at their best in this early phase? Has there been conflict? If yes, how have they dealt with it? Have they been intimate emotionally as well as physically and do they know the difference yet? In the not too distant future the fabric of the relationship will be tested. As the profile of one party interfaces with the biography of the other party, will they be able to reconcile their differences with open communication, trust and mutual respect for each other's wishes, needs and desires? Or, when they enter the "real phase" of the relationship, will the romantic phase have been proven to be an illusion?

Forgiveness, like romance, kindness, honesty and openness, is another virtue that is highly valued by society. However, *false forgiveness*, in my view, is a major gaffe in significant relationships that can contribute to superficial and artificial anxiety-laden interactions if the relationships in question do survive. When individuals forgive just to forgive because it is the nice and proper thing to do—and for that reason only—they are in denial of the feelings that created the schism in the first place. Or, worse, they are aware of those feelings and are not articulating them to the other party. We all know the tension in the air when we "sit on" unresolved feelings in the presence of someone who hurt us while pretending everything is alright. On the other hand *true forgiveness* relieves such tension and when both parties communicate their feelings openly and directly, in the process they learn about each other's sensibilities.

Finally, *sincerity*, in one sense, is also overrated. Many people state intentions as promises and they mean what they say at the time they say it (even politicians can be sincere . . . I think). New information however can alter the circumstances that created the (faulty) impression that the person was being phony all along. A second related reason for not idealizing the concept of sincerity is that there are occasions in which a person is being sincere but is not in complete control of the emotions underlying the sincerity. For example, Andrea, with some hesitancy, was sincere when she agreed with Bud that they would live together without being married. Andrea had taken the position that in her culture (Latina) marriage and love were practically synonymous, a belief that conflicted with her reality that she felt deeply loved by Bud even though they were not married. Bud (Jewish), more of an independent thinker, would tease Andrea: "If I still followed my cultural belief I would be a rabbi instead of an entertainer." Andrea gave up her apartment and Bud made provisions for her financially in case he could no longer work or if he died. Andrea asked Bud to pick up a gift card for friends who were getting married. When she came home she read the card out loud to Bud with great emphasis: "When a man and woman truly love each other . . . their special day . . ." She kept reading the card over and over and with each read her voice got louder and louder. Finally she said to Bud, "Don't you get it?" In time, it became clear that Andrea's strong cultural conviction outweighed her sincere intentions to move in with Bud without demanding marriage. Bud felt betrayed and the relationship ended.

In truth, most well-intentioned people among us cannot be real all the time. Throwing caution to the wind with unbridled expression of affect (being constantly open and honest) can be harmful, embarrassing and dangerous at times. Endless romance, frivolous forgiveness and efforts at sincerity are likewise not foolproof. The best we can do is to be ourselves as much as possible, a goal challenging enough because of our imperfections and complex nature.

The most honest, forgiving, sincere, kind person I ever knew was my beloved mother, Sally—talk about honest and direct! She once told a girlfriend of mine upon their first meeting that she was much too young for me. "I don't like this arrangement; you better not hurt my son," she said. Another example of her kindness and sincerity took place at a supermarket. We were at the frozen food section when she spotted a man at the checkout counter with his pants hanging down and his buttocks exposed. She was embarrassed for him and approached him. She said, "Excuse me, sir, but your behind is sticking out." The man in a gruff voice said, "So what business is it of yours?" My mother replied, "You should not speak to me in that manner and if you don't apologize I'll kick you where the sun don't shine." Talk about real!

GLOSSARY

Abandonment. An action of physical and/or emotional distancing on the part of a caregiver that causes severe anxiety and shocks the system of a young child or adult.

The Caretaker Contract. An unstated agreement generated by the unconscious mind of the caretaker and others presumably for the benefit of both parties concerned.

Combined Individual and Group Therapy. The concurrent application of individual and group therapy by the same therapist that is distinguished from *conjoint therapy* that involves a different therapist for each modality.

Cryogenics. The science of freezing a body part for future transplants. A metaphor used to describe the "freeze effect" of psychological trauma that impedes the separation (from early influences) process.

Emotional/Sexual Celibacy. Self-imposed denial of need gratification that can be a choice or a compulsion that serves a protective function (mask).

Generalization. The tendency to imbue most, if not all, current adult experiences with reminiscences of past traumatic events and emotions associated with them.

Guilt by Design. An automatic reflex that reinforces the caretaker pattern designed by the psychological immune system as a protection from reexperiencing anxiety and other painful emotions.

Harmony of the Personality. The integration of the parts of the personality that were frozen by trauma with the whole personality; the hallmark of recovery and cure.

Horizontal Attachment. A more equal position relative to others and one "measure" of recovery.

Invisibility. The unbearable experience of being ignored that motivates the entire caretaker syndrome including the relentless pursuit of contact by pleasing, irrespective of consequences (e.g., emotional deprivation, unfulfilling relationships).

Mask. A metaphor used to describe both benign (adaptive) and pathological (maladaptive) behavior in a social context.

Mask of Kindness. A persona "invented" by the psychological immune system that incorporates selflessness at its core in order to neutralize the memory and emotions associated with trauma.

Path Diagram. A visual snapshot that depicts the path of self-focus and detours that are associated with guilt.

Psychological Immune System. A hypothetical inborn system analogous to the biological immune system that provides protection from psychological harm. The system's components include somatization, defenses, character traits and masks.

Psychological Trauma. Emotional shock that tests the limits of the psychological immune system by devastating its victims into a state of helplessness, terror and fears of annihilation.

Rebuilding. A psychological and emotional reconstruction of the personality following the intentional disassembling (through therapy, etc.) or unintentional obliteration (breakdown) of the mask of kindness.

Recovery Process. (a) The relief of symptoms of the caretaker personality disorder that is characterized by significantly reduced anxiety associated with anticipated abandonment, emotional distancing, neglect and abuse; *(b)* The reduction of selfless acts motivated for a self-serving purpose that guarantees the presence of others and serves as a "quick fix" for heightened self-esteem. *(c)* The establishment of genuine relationships with authentic communication, empathy and self-disclosure.

Retraining. The ofttimes tedious process of teaching and reteaching others that the mask of kindness has been removed and replaced by interactions that entail mutuality, reciprocity and an improved give-receive balance.

Selflessness. A specific trait addiction that is socially redeeming that is characterized by both excessive giving and discomfort and avoidance of receiving from others.

Tolerance. The state of please addicts wherein supplies need to be increased because of their insatiable need to be needed by others that represents the ultimate diversion from their concealed inner turmoil.

Trait Addiction. An unconscious compulsion to hook onto a character trait, e.g. selflessness (in contrast to a substance or activity) as a substitute for other sources of gratification the care addict is too anxious to pursue.

Trauma Zone. Any event or emotion associated with reminiscences of a past shock trauma that has the power to contaminate current experiences.

True Self. The spontaneous, natural essence of the caretaker that lies beneath the mask that seeks, but fears, exposure.

Vertical Attachment. A metaphor that describes the position caretakers assume relative to others in order to maintain control and distance.

REFERENCES

Barbanell, L. *Removing the Mask of Kindness: Diagnosis and Treatment of the Caretaker Personality Disorder.* Lanham, MD: Jason Aronson, 2006.

Berglas, S. *The Success Syndrome.* New York: Plenum Press, 1986.

Fraiberg, S. *The Magic Years.* New York: Fireside/Simon & Schuster, 1959.

Levinson, D. *The Seasons of Man's Life.* New York: Aspen/Ballantine Books, 1986.

Packard, V. *Hidden Persuaders.* New York: Simon & Schuster, 1957.

Reich, W. *Character Analysis.* New York: Touchstone Books, 1974.

Webster's New World Dictionary and Thesaurus. 2nd ed. Cleveland: Wiley, 2002.

INDEX

abandonment, 92
addiction, 2; to please, 6; psychotherapists and, 80
Allen, Woody, 35
altruism, 4
analysis, relational, 83

benign states: of psychotherapists, 81
Bradshaw, Terry, 34
Brando, Marlon, 33
burnout, 5

Caretaker Personality Disorder (CPD), 5; and caring, 76–77; criteria for, 6–8; deception and, 66; histories of, 88; matches/mismatches, 9; relationships, 12; pseudo-connections, 70
Carnegie, Andrew, 47
Cirque du Soleil, 18
Cobain, Kurt, 33
codependence, 5
compassion, 4
contract, hidden, 123–*124*

defense mechanisms, 22; tense, 27
denial, 22
Diana, Princess, 47
displacement, 22–23
distancing, emotional, 39, 93

emotions, bodyguard of, 18
empathy, 5

forgiveness, 148
Fraiberg, Salma, 57

generalizations, 57
geometric reconfiguration, 100
Gibble, Matthew, 19
give-receive chart, 126–127
guilt and anxiety, 72, 106

harmony, 144
The Hidden Persuaders, 15
honesty, 147

illusion of closeness, 65
immune system, psychological, 16; components of, 17–18

Jackson, Michael, 34
Jordan, Michael, 19, 35

Keaton, Diane, 35
Kelly, Gene, 39
Karnazes, Dean, 19
kindness, 147

masks: of athletic prowess, 24; of celebrity, 32–33; of celibacy, 35–37; emptiness and, 53–54; of fame, 32–34; multiple, 37; of physical attractiveness, 32–33; of success, 31
masochism, 5
Mason, Jackie, 30
Monroe, Marilyn, 33
Mother Teresa. *See* Teresa, Mother

narcissism, 66; and selflessness, *67*
Navratilova, Martina, 35
Newman, Paul, 40
Nightingale, Florence, 46

obligation checklist, 125–*126*

Packard, Vance, 15
pathological states, of psychotherapists, 82
Perry, Bob, 34
Pilobolus, 18
Presley, Elvis, 34
projection, 22
psychotherapists and CPD, 80–81
psychotherapy, 129; group, 130

rationalization, 23
reaction formation, 23

reality, biographical, 60; current, 60
rebuilding, 122
recovery, obstacles to, 112–116, 136
repression, 22
retraining, of others, 134
Rodriguez, Alex, 34

self: the lost, 99; true, 99
self-focus, path to, 128
selflessness, 2; definition of, 3, 104; personality scale, 105
sincerity, 149
Sinatra, Frank, 39
sublimation, 23

Teresa, Mother, 47
trauma, 90; abandonment, 92; detection of, 98; emotional, 93; nature of, 91; sexual, 95

unconscious, 13; janus-faced, 15; nature of, 14

Wood, Natalie, 39
Woods, Tiger, 35

ABOUT THE AUTHOR

Les Barbanell received his doctoral degree from Columbia University and did his postdoctoral training at the Postgraduate Center for Mental Health in New York City (group therapy program) and the New Jersey Institute for Training in Teaneck, New Jersey, where he is a faculty member, supervisor and training analyst. His book *Removing the Mask of Kindness: Diagnosis and Treatment of the Caretaker Personality Disorder* was published by Jason Aronson in 2006. He formulated the concept "caretaker personality disorder" in 2006, and his concept "psychological immune system" (discussed in this book and elsewhere) is also an original formulation. Other publications include articles on narcissism, selflessness, sports, adolescence and relationships. He has a general practice in Englewood Cliffs, New Jersey, and specializes in psychotherapy for helping professionals, including therapists, physicians, nurses, clergymen and counselors.

Barbanell annually presents six-week seminars in relational analysis to psychologists, social workers and psychiatrists. He is an active member of the National Association for the Advancement of Psychoanalysis and the New Jersey Psychological Association. He is a diplomat of the American Psychotherapy Association. He resides in Fort Lee, New Jersey. For more information, visit his website, psychologistdynam.com, or e-mail him at empathman@ aol.com.

Breinigsville, PA USA
07 May 2010
237528BV00003B/1/P